Talk to Me

By David Burrows

Destiny Image Publishers
P.O. Box 310
Shippensburg, PA 17257-0351

"We Publish the Prophets"

ISBN 1-56043-086-9

For Worldwide Distribution
Printed in the U.S.A.

Contents

Dedication

To my wife Angie and children Arri and Davrielle, my greatest joys in life.

To my mom, without whom I probably would never have made it.

To my dad, whom I have come to know after my years of rebellion.

To my immediate family, #1 to #7 (brothers and sisters).

Especially to my spiritual big brothers Myles Munroe and Robyn Gool.

To the gang at Live Youth and BFM.

Acknowledgments

It's been a long road from the time I was a youngster who didn't have a sense of direction, growing up wanting to be a criminal, spending time on the street and believing, "This is life."

Warren Street and Harlem (where I hung out as a youth in Nassau, Bahamas), taught me things about life that I could not possibly have gotten out of any book. My experiences on the street left scars on my mind that will never go away, yet I'm grateful to have been there and to understand, from the inside as a participant, what the mind of those on the other side of life is. Perhaps it would have been better if I had grown up in church, but I got there as a street person, into drugs and in the fast and dangerous lane. I will never forget the street, or as we would say, the "blocks."

I am grateful to all those to whom I dedicated this work, but especially to Robyn Gool, Myles Munroe and Dorcas Burrows (my mother). These are the people God used most to transform Dave "Davy B" Burrows from a street mind headed for destruction into a man with a purpose and a direction that cannot change or be lost.

For the development and production of this book, I am grateful to:

My wife Angela and my children Arri and Davrielle. Angie, you are my inspiration for everything I do well. Thanks for believing in me and encouraging me.

The gang at BFM and especially Live Youth—Tellis "Aqua Man" Bethel, Teri Bethel, David and Florrie Knowles—and the LIVE YOUTH who keep us working as we see ours and their potential realized.

The directors of BFM who have tolerated a wild and crazy guy like me on their board.

Myles Munroe, who always encourages me to be the best I can be.

Foreword

"Nobody understands me." These famous words have probably been spoken by all teenagers—or they have filled their thoughts—no matter what the culture, race or creed of the youths. In most cases, they are uttered in frustration because of a confrontation with authority, be it with a parent, a guardian, a teacher or some other adult. It is amazing how quickly adults forget their teenage years and the struggles of their journeys through that frightening no man's land called adolescence.

The teenage years are probably the most difficult time of life because they are that critical period of transition when the individual moves through the stormy waters and the rites of passage from childhood to adulthood. Characterized by intense grappling with internal, external, physiological, emotional and psychological changes, these years are the time when values, morals, standards and boundaries are tested and stretched to the limit. Being a teenager is difficult, especially in a world that is designed for adults. For many teenagers, this experience is so traumatic that it leaves life-long scars that dramatically affect their entire lives.

The teenage years are also difficult and challenging for a child's parents and the other significant adults in his or her life. They often find it difficult to accept the child's increasingly independent behavior as he or she looks to other sources for reference, counsel and influence. In their desire to maintain control, parents often lash out against that which they do not fully understand. Insensitivity and irrationality frequently influence their responses. This occurs because most adults do not remember the changes and experiences that were part of their own teenage years, nor do they understand their child's world.

While it is true that the process of development is basically the same for all teens, it is essential to note that each generation confronts challenges and social situations that are unique to their generation. Clothes, hair styles, music, entertainment, language, sports, movies and status symbols all have a slightly different manifestation that those experienced by a teen's parents or grandparents. Many adults do not take the time to discover these differences so they can understand the culture of their teenager. Therefore, they fail to appreciate the tremendously complex world in which their child lives.

This ignorance is often at the root of the power struggles that many teens and their parents experience. Therefore, it is important for parents and other adults who desire to help teens through this period of transition to be aware that many of their perceptions of youth and their world are misconceptions. Consider the following examples: A teenager's attempt to improve his decision-making skills and to develop an independent assessment of life may be seen by adults as rebellion. Or an adolescent's desire to exercise his social skills and to reinforce his self-concept by establishing relationships with his peers may be interpreted as wild and loose living. Likewise, a teenager's attempt to develop responsibility is likely to be translated as a deliberate, willful attempt to go against the wishes of his parents or guardians. Such misunderstandings arise primarily because adults do not have a full awareness of the tremendous complexities that face their young adults. The resulting conflicts can be transformed into enlightening experiences if both the teenager and his or her parents make the effort to understand that they are striving for the same goal.

David Burrows sets out in this book a comprehensive but simple presentation of both the dynamics at work in the teenage years and the principles that underlie many of the potential conflicts between youth and adults. By examining the problems and challenges that youth face—such as drug abuse, AIDS, sex, music, fashions, friendships and self-esteem—and by providing simple, time-tested answers, Dave shows youth how to effectively meet each challenge with confidence. Youth counselors and parents who wish to understand the complex nature of their teenagers will find this book to be a manual that better equips them to respond effectively during these critical years. Dave's practical, simple and sound style will help them to recall their own teenage years and, thus, will enable them to identify with today's youth.

Dave's years of working with youth are evident in his candid approach to the challenges youth encounter. He draws both on his experiences as an administrator in the youth department of the Bahamas government and the insight he has gained through his present position as the youth pastor of Bahamas Faith Ministries. Every teenager will see himself in Dave's experiences. He or she will also profit from the clear, biblical principles and counsel that Dave presents to help youth make that essential journey from childhood to adulthood a safe, beneficial transition that will serve as an anchor for the children of tomorrow. Read and enjoy a book that will become a classic for years to come as you stay...forever young.

Dr. Myles Munroe
Nassau, Bahamas

Young people everywhere are struggling with identity, acceptance, relationship with parents, sex, crime, academics and the list goes on. Parents everywhere are struggling with understanding their teenagers, communicating with them, being able role models and the list goes on. Is there an answer?

A recent study stated that teenagers are influenced most by television, peers, school, family and church, in that order. No wonder there are over 400,000 teenage suicides every year. No wonder teenage pregnancy is at an all time high. No wonder there are so many teenage runaways. No wonder over 58% of our youth have tried marijuana, the list goes on. Is there an answer?

I believe that in this book teenagers and parents will find the hope, direction and insight that both will need to help turn these disturbing statistics around. There is an answer.

Dave Burrows has drawn from experiences on "both sides of the fence," the Spirit of God and the Word of God, and several years of working with youth to compile principles, concepts and standards that will change the course of our youth, on their relationship with their parents. Every parent would do themselves a favor by reading and implementing the principles and practical suggestions that are given.

I have known Dave for over 18 years, before he accepted the King of Kings. In fact, God allowed me to be an instrument in his conversion. It is true when Paul wrote by the Spirit "from glory to glory." David Burrows over the years literally changed from a drug user and dealer, a man on the "blocks", to a committed, dedicated, anointed man of God, called to minister to our youth. To help give direction and bridge gaps found in the family because of the works of darkness. You will thoroughly enjoy the practical way this book is written, flavored by personal experience and loaded with the power of God.

My prayer is that the eyes of your understanding will be enlightened, and the Spirit of God will show everyone that picks up this book that there is an answer.

Pastor Robyn Gool
Victory Christian Center
Charlotte, North Carolina

Preface

It is difficult to sit on the sidelines and see young people being drawn to their death by a spiritual and physical world that is out of order. It is even more difficult when you know the answers and find it hard to communicate those answers to the mass of young people who fall by the wayside every day.

I realized that I had to put into print what I had come to know as the truth not from a secondhand point of view, but from the belly of the beast. You see, I grew up as a rebellious youth who learned all the wrong things about life. I learned to cuss, to fight, to sell drugs, to take drugs and to abuse women for selfish gain. I learned these things not from a book, but firsthand. As I was introduced to the real truth about life, I came to appreciate how deceptive and cunning satan really is. He takes truth and makes it appear a lie and takes a lie and makes it appear as truth. So I had to expose what had happened to me and what is still happening to millions of young people every day.

I know we can change the world. I know we can change what is happening with young people. But somebody has to say it, write it, play it, teach it, show it, do it over and over again because teens are like wet cement—very impressionable and easily moved. What they experience at that stage of life is very often fixed in their personalities and difficult to alter. So if we do it right the first time, we will not have to do it over again.

Teenagers are the future and they must know the truth about the issues of life. One of the saddest commentaries on today's church is that we so often do everything possible to run youth away from our doors. We tell them what we like and what our program is and let them know that if they don't fit into that mold, they shouldn't even enter the doors. These attitudes must change.

We must realize that some things about teenagers will never change, but as time passes, the way it is communicated or played out will change. What worked five or ten years ago may not be applicable today. We should watch and listen so we can understand how to best meet their needs. Eventually we must turn the keys over to them, so why not prepare them for the roles they will fill by doing only what is right? Invite them to show us how we can assist them in a way they understand and relate to.

I hope this book will give us all a better view of the issues teenagers and young adults face and provide us with the answers to understand life and what God desires us to do better. The Bible is the road map. It is our constitution. If we look closely and read carefully, we will understand that God is not only cool, He is awesome. He is the One who designed life and the One who knows how it should operate. In the words of a song by the young rappers, System 3, He is:

> The Master,
> The one true blaster
> Knows how to make things
> Slower or faster

1 What's Wrong with Today's Teenagers

Children crying
Babies dying
Government officials
Always lying
Is there hope
Is God real
Why do people cheat and steal

I know there's something Better
I know there has to be
I know there's something more
Than Reality

I'm searching for a Better Way
In Life
I know there's a Better Way
...Jesus is the Better Way

(System 3) Used by permission.

Today's Realities

"Welcome to the six o'clock news. In our top story today, a teenager murders his twelve-year-old brother because he could not use his brother's bicycle. On the other side of town, a seventeen-year-old high school student was arrested for having possession of twenty kilos of coke and is alleged to have developed a network of young pushers who sold drugs in schools. At the time of his arrest, he was driving a brand new BMW and wearing a Rolex watch that is worth a year's salary for some. And finally, a young lady just fifteen-years-old had her second child today in St. PM's hospital...."

In case you haven't noticed, this world is out of order and the purpose and meaning of life is apparently unknown. The further along we go, the farther away we seem to get from God's original design and purpose. Although the problems of today actually have a very simple solution, humans are too "smart." They spend their time creating their own inventions rather than returning to the Maker and asking Him for the specifications on which life should operate. God has the answer for everything because He created everything. God had a design, a plan for this world and all the things in it. However, things are not what they should be. The following note indicates what is wrong with us as human beings. Although it was written years ago, it still applies to today's world.

> For although they knew God, they neither glorified him as God nor gave thanks to him, but their thinking became futile and their foolish hearts were darkened. Although they claimed to be wise, they became fools and exchanged the glory of the immortal God for images made to look like mortal man and birds and animals and reptiles. Therefore God gave them over in the sinful desires of their hearts to sexual impurity.... They exchanged the truth of God for a lie, and worshiped and served created things rather than the Creator... (Romans 1:21-25).

Something is indeed wrong with our world. If you were to ask for my opinion, I would have to tell you that this world is a mess in general and specifically a mess in regards to teenagers.

Why are youth doing the things they do and behaving the way they behave? If you can add in simple math, I can tell you right now. Youth today must grow up in a world that teaches sex outside of marriage is not only okay, it is imperative. These young people grow up learning that life doesn't matter much. They see people blown away every day on television. Murder is a part of life, and is even used as entertainment on television and in movies. So, when they have a problem, they think about violence.

Some people in our society are alarmed at the level of violence among teenagers and they keep asking, "Why?" If you can add one plus one and get two, you should be smart enough to discover what is wrong with teenagers. In this equation, one point is they watch it all day. Add the fact that the violent, macho guys we see are portrayed as heroes. Then we should understand that adding one plus one equals two: They go out and do it. When teenagers have a problem, they become the superhero they saw in the movies who can defeat a whole army and walk away with just a few scratches. The only thing they fail to realize is that only happens in the movies.

Don't believe just me; think of how many times lately you saw or heard a young person called the nickname of one of the heroes or villains from a recent gangster movie. Have you noticed the violence that follows movies about gangs or movies with violent themes? If it's on the movie screen today, it will be on the streets tomorrow. You don't need a degree to figure that out. Murder is often glorified; "hit man" is a popular heroic term; violence is entertainment. It's in the music and on the TV screen; then it shows up at school or on the basketball court.

I have a son just six years old. My son will watch wrestling for one minute, then come at me with a popular wrestling move the next. The values presented to teenagers every day leads them further and further away from God's design and, not coincidentally, toward suicide, AIDS and death. Our society continues to practice values that ruin young people. Teenage ladies try to see who can be the "sexiest." At one time it was a real scandal for a single young lady to not be a virgin. Now it is almost a crime to be one. Teenagers end up using drugs and becoming involved in a variety of drug-related activities. Although they can choose and make their own decisions about their futures, the world they meet is weighted against their future success.

Teenagers don't go to Colombia and fly drugs across the Atlantic for sale and distribution. Teenagers don't write television shows or movies. They are indelibly influenced by what is written and done by adults.

How many young ladies get pregnant or engage in premarital sex because the values presented by society teach that sex is fun and okay "if you love someone," or even if you don't. If you watch MTV and check out the latest music videos, that message is clearly expressed in the words of popular songs like "I Want to Sex You Up." The commercials on television many times don't sell products, they sell sex in order to sell the product. How irresponsible can society get?

If people want to know what is wrong with today's teenagers, they must look at parents and society as a whole. The world that has been shaped for teenagers is full of drugs (the one in the bottle or the one in the can), sex, crime and apathy. Some young people drink beer, others smoke grass. Some hit coke, others discover the tragedies of AIDS, teenage pregnancy and abortion. They are victims of a world that is, in many respects, lost and without hope (except for the fact that something better does exist, and they just don't know it). Of course, even though you young people may be victims of circumstances, that does not mean you are bound by those circumstances forever. There is a better way, if you would choose to find it.

Broken People Produce Broken Families Which Produce Broken Teenagers

Many teenagers do not know what a family is. They grow up in a smorgasbord of relationships which do not give any clear indication of stability. Some families have one parent; some have two parents but one is there only in name; some grow up in families with two women or two men; some have revolving fathers or revolving mothers. Divorce is often a discussed reality among teens. Just the other day I conducted a survey of my church teenagers to find out how many have two parents at home who are faithful to each other, as far as these teens knew. The shocking result was something like 25 percent of those questioned. It seems the majority of teens today grow up in households that are either single-parented or dysfunctional. It can't be strange for teenagers to consider suicide when they live in a world like that and were never exposed to real truth. It can't be surprising that some of them want to run away. Wouldn't you?

What Happened to Our Heroes?

Politicians, public officials and sports figures are implicated in scandal after scandal. One week they come and address a school assembly about hard work and morals and the next week they are in court or in the news for corruption or sexual deviance. "Magic Johnson has AIDS" is the headline in the news. We are told that he didn't discriminate much about women and sex; it was available and he took advantage of it. Magic obviously has tremendous talent and is a great inspiration to all those who watch him. But what does something like that say to us?

Politicians who campaign for the high office of President lie to the public and get caught by the media, who never did believe what they said. Then there are preachers and "reverends" molesting children, having affairs, lying, cheating and stealing. How is a teenager to make sense out of this? We thought the church would be the last to disappoint us. Such is the world we live in today. It is the world in which teenagers must grow up.

Today's Teens: Tomorrow's Parents, Tomorrow's Leaders

A lot is wrong with today's teenagers. They are more violent, are sexually active at earlier ages, have less respect for parents, are more likely to drop out of school and are generally malcontent. Of course that does not apply to all teenagers. But suffice it to say that, taken as a whole, these are the facts of life. However, when trying to discover what is wrong with today's youth, we need to look at today's parents.

Parents today work more, spend less time with their children, are more likely to divorce and remarry several times or are single parents, and are one of the primary causes for the state of their children. The Bible talks about sowing and reaping, seed time and harvest: "As long as the earth endures, seedtime and harvest...will never cease"

(Genesis 8:22). What society sees in teenagers today is a reflection of what happened yesterday.

If parents want to know what is wrong with their children, they should look in the mirror of their lives and multiply what they see.

Whatever you as a parent do and however you live, some, if not all, of your children will end up just like you. Parents must realize that children often take what exists in their parents and add to it. Parents should be careful how they live in front of their teenagers.

The words in a popular song of some years ago underscores this point so clearly:

The cat's in the cradle and the silver spoon,
little boy blue and the man in the moon,
when you comin home dad I don't know when,
but we'll get together then dad,
you know we'll have a good time then...
...As I hung up the phone it occurred to me
The boy was just like me yea, he was just like me.

This exact sentiment is being repeated all over the world, day after day.

Seeds Sown; Harvest Reaped

To one who knows the Bible, it is obvious that this world is not functioning in the way it was designed. It is out of order just like your phone can be out of order and not work. It may irritate you to call a friend and hear a recording that says, "We're sorry; the number you have dialed is out of order." Now think of this world as being out of order.

This world has been and continues to be out of order. God never designed the mess we are in now. Man put this ship together. How much is this world out of order? Consider this: We put a warning on cigarettes, which help people kill themselves, but don't put a warning on alcohol, which kills so many more. Have you ever seen someone come home and beat up his wife because he had a cigarette? Yet people emphasize and lobby for the prohibition of cigarettes while allowing the foremost drug in the world unrestricted access to our airwaves. It seems to me that alcohol kills more people both directly and indirectly than any other drug. So if cigarettes are banned, what will happen to alcohol? Our drug problem today came from the alcohol seed sown by our parents.

**The world today is reaping a bitter harvest.
This harvest is born of parents in
an irresponsible society and reaped
in teenagers who are out of order.**

Remember this: Every time an act of adultery is committed, a seed is planted that *will* bear fruit. It's the law of the universe. If some child is raised without a father or mother, chances are he or she will grow up deficiently and produce offspring that grow up in the same manner and with the same result. Every time another bottle of beer is sold, a seed is planted. Every time we hear "This Bud's for you," another young man believes he can pass into adulthood only if he drinks beer. Every prisoner put in jail is a harvest of something that happened to that person years ago. But before he or she is safely behind bars, that person's harvest has planted seeds that will take their place in society.

What is wrong with today's teenagers is what we adults all are. What we see in them is really us. This picture may seem gruesome, and it is. But does that mean there is no hope? Certainly not! Stick around and read on; there is a solution.

Has a Generation Been Lost?

Even though the picture I have just painted actually exists today, a generation of youth has not been lost. We have and are losing many, many young people, but we have not lost a generation. In every city there are young people who know and who refuse to bow to the idols of the day. They refuse to accept a disconnected society. They searched for and found the truth in a Book and in the life of the Author of the Book. A new and bold generation is rising up today. They have a purpose; they have goals in life; they refuse to bow down to the idols I mentioned earlier. There are still Daniels, Shadrachs, Meschachs and Abednegos, Timothys, Davids and countless others who would rather burn than bow. But they are convinced they will not have to burn because they know that God is on their side and if He is for you, who can be against you?

Yes, a lot of young people have been lost, but this generation has not been lost. God always has a people who know the truth—young and old, rich and poor, bold and beautiful—who have already decided that they will make the difference. These young people have learned about their purpose for living. They have developed a relationship with the Creator. They have determined their destination and know what it takes to get there. They have examined the facts and concluded that Jesus is the answer, that God knows them better than they know themselves and that if they follow His commands, they will have true success.

Points to Remember

---

1. Teenagers don't go to Columbia and fly drugs across the Atlantic for sale and distribution.

2. Teenagers don't write television shows or movies.

3. Teenagers are indelibly influenced by what is written and done by adults.

4. If parents want to know what is wrong with their children, they should look in the mirror of their lives and multiply what they see.

5. The world today is reaping a bitter harvest. This harvest is born of parents in an irresponsible society and reaped in teenagers who are out of order.

6. There are still Daniels, Shadrachs, Meschachs and Abednegos, Timothys, Davids and countless others who know the truth, who will go with God and who will make the difference.

2 | Parents and Teens Face Off

Mommy's crying
Daddy's gone
Mommy is no longer
singing a song
I hurt so bad inside
with you not by my side
Mommy and Daddy
Please hear my cry

Love the Children
Give us a chance
We are tomorrow
We deserve a chance...

(Written by Ms. Debbie Bartlett) Used by permission.

Whatever Happened to the Thing Called Family?

What or who is a parent or parents? What or who is a family? There was a time when these questions were easily answered, but as we look around us we see that times have changed. There was a time when parents meant a father and mother who were married and had children who carried the same name and characteristics of their parents. Today it is hard to identify what a family is.

Many young people cannot identify with the illustrations in the Bible that deal with father and son. They don't quite understand what it means to have a real father to whom they can relate.

That is why it is so wrong to have illegitimate children. These children must grow up either sharing a father or having no father or mother at all. Society is full of one-parent homes or homes where one parent is there in name only. We pay a high price for this situation. It is the children who suffer the most.

We as church people often hear teachings on husbands and wives, but rarely do we hear teachings about parents and children; particularly teenagers. These problems are so significant, society has coined some new terms like "the generation gap." Many teens have problems relating to parents, and parents to teens. Some parents can't cope. Some teens can't cope. What can be done?

As early as in the Book of Genesis God asks an interesting question. "Adam, where are you?" Of course He knew where Adam was, but He was asking the question for Adam's (man's) sake. God was saying, "Mr. Head of the House, where are you? Are you in the position you should be or not? What happened to your family?"

What Happened to Daddy and Mommy?

There was a time when children learned about life from their parents. Mommy was the role model for little Susie;

Daddy was the role model for little Johnny. Mommy would take Susie under her care and teach her how to be a lady. Susie would learn how to cook, sew and take care of certain things around the house as she watched Mommy. She would learn how to dress and fix her hair and when it was time, Mommy would sit Susie down and tell her about, as it is called, "the birds and the bees." Meanwhile Daddy would take little Johnny and show him how to be a man, playing ball with him and being his hero. Johnny would say, "I wanna be like you, Dad. You know I want to be like you." Little boys used to be proud of their fathers; they played ball together and Daddy pointed Johnny in the right direction. But oh, how times have changed.

What often happens today is that Daddy left a long time ago. He has children here and around the corner, sometimes in the next state or the next country. He may telephone once in awhile or even visit, but little Johnny doesn't care anymore. He thinks Daddy is a jerk, a no good bum and a waste. He doesn't care if Daddy comes again or not. Johnny has already gone through the pain of not having a father and at this point he is too bitter to care. He now identifies with the boys.

So often today Mommy is the only parent. Daddy left some time ago with his young secretary and is no longer around. So Mommy works two jobs just so she and the children can survive. She ends up being a role model for Johnny and Susie not by choice, but by default. Mommy does not really have time to teach the children anything; she leaves them with the television and a babysitter and goes off to work to make sure they have a reasonable lifestyle.

Who or What Is Daddy and Mommy?

Sometimes the situation is even more confused. Johnny has two daddies, Susie has two mommies. Mommy's husband is another woman. Or, it may be that after Daddy left,

Mommy's boyfriend moved in. He molests Susie, but Susie won't talk because she believes Mommy will get mad and no one will believe her.

It is interesting to note that when Paul wrote the Book of Ephesians, he assumed he was addressing families with both father and mother. Notice he said, "Children, obey your parents" (6:1). Today this parental relationship may mean only 30 to 40 percent of the population.

What is a family? If Paul were writing the Book of Ephesians today, he would have to say, "Children, obey your parents, your guardians, your step-parents, the man who lives in the house or your grandmother." A family can be almost any strange combination. Unfortunately, we of today must learn to deal with one-parent families, step-families, absentee parents, parents who visit and parents who send their regards.

However, problems still exist even when both parents are home. Parents begin to say, "How do I deal with this lousy teen? She used to be so sweet. Now all we do is argue and fight." At one time Susie thought the world of Mommy, but now she doesn't want Mommy to pick her up from the party. She no longer agrees with Mommy's view of the world.

Other parents refuse to spend time with their children. They are too busy making important career moves or making moves on co-workers to pay any attention to their children. So they send money or buy more toys to satisfy their anxious teen. What's the solution?

How Do Teens and Parents Get Along?

God's original plan for the family was one man, one woman and their children (Genesis 2:24). The man was responsible under God. The woman was responsible as partner and helper. Both were responsible for teaching their children and providing love, discipline and respect. The Bible shows us what was originally intended for the family.

> **For this reason a man will leave his father and mother and be united to his wife, and the two will become one flesh** (Ephesians 5:31).

> **Children, obey your parents in the Lord, for this is right. "Honor your father and mother"—which is the first commandment with a promise—"that it may go well you and that you may enjoy long life on the earth." Fathers, do not exasperate your children; instead, bring them up in the training and instruction of the Lord** (Ephesians 6:1-4).

The plan was simple. A man and his wife would live together, love each other and bring up children, passing on to their children the instructions God had given. This plan was interrupted by the fall, the disobedience of man. Man became separated from God, so the family was also disconnected from God. Man forgot, or no longer understood, the purpose God had for the family. Naturally, where purpose is not known, abuse is inevitable.

Man abused the very thing God had designed to protect him and to give him the stability he needs to survive. Drastic consequences have resulted. Further destruction is now taking place. Can you imagine growing up in a home where two women live together as a man and woman should? God's original plan can hardly be recognized in today's world. In the Book of Genesis, not too long after the first family existed, God could no longer confidently deal with any family unit. The Bible says He had to search for a man who would teach his children.

> **For I have chosen him, so that he will direct his children and his household after him to keep the way of the Lord by doing what is right and just, so that the Lord will bring about for Abraham what he has promised him** (Genesis 18:19).

God had to search for a man who would teach his family. Does that remind you of anything? God thinks it is important for families to work right. If even one link is missing, there is potential for chaos.

What Am I Supposed to Do?

When examining the problem and the solution, we need to look at the roles of both parties. What should a parent be doing? What should a child be doing? What was God's purpose and design for parents and children, particularly teenagers and young adults? Let's deal with the nature and role of each.

What Is the Nature or Makeup of Youth?

a) Teens want their own identity.

Parents become used to having little Susie or little Johnny follow them everywhere they go, believe everything they say, look up to them for advice and tell them everything that happens in school. But parents get one of their biggest shocks after little Susie or little Johnny reach the age of thirteen. All of a sudden the sky that was blue all along, without question, is no longer blue. Little Susie or little Johnny comes home and says, "You know what, Mommy, I believe the sky is green." Or they may say, "I don't see why

I can't have sex if I want to." Mom and Dad have the shock of their lives and the war is on.

> **The fact is, all teens want to establish their own identity. They want to form their own ideas, apart from their parents.**

Parents already have their identity. They have been through that process. If the situation is handled rightly, parents can help kids answer their questions and help them form the proper identity. But if handled wrongly, it can mean disaster. Lines of communication break down and a wall is raised for several years. Statements like "Don't drop me off at school; I can take care of myself" are not against parents. Teens are really saying, "I want to be more responsible for my own affairs and I want to identify with my peers."

b) Teens develop their own language and culture.

Not too long ago parents themselves were teens. They spoke a language that was "in" for that time. The language has changed today. Often parents, already through this phase, are out of touch with today's language and culture.

> **Parents must contend with new words and phrases that are already set in today's teen world and culture. These are words that parents have not heard of nor understand the meaning of.**

This language barrier results in blocked communication.

Another aspect of teen culture is hairstyles. Years ago, house wars began when a teen came home with shoulder-length hair or an Afro. Parents just didn't understand. Now guys may wear pony tails, earrings in their ears, weird hair-cuts and other fashions that are often just statements of independence and changing styles. We must face one thing: Most teens think their parents are "uncool" or "out of touch."

c) Teenagers are idealistic.

Teens are full of idealism. It happens in every genera-tion. Teens believe that they can change the world and that they have new ideas different and better than those of their parents. Teens look for a better existence and are critical of existing institutions. "We can make it better (do it better, make a change)."

Much of what happened in past years was a statement from a younger generation also believing that something was wrong with the existing society and its institutions and that they could change it and make it better. Every genera-tion sees new ideas developing from a new generation of youth. Some of these have been positive and some negative, but the fact that young people try to change the world will always be a part of youth.

d) Teens are full of energy.

A teen is full of unbridled energy. They are always look-ing for what's happening, wanting to party, wanting to have a good time, looking for something to do. Kids are always saying, "What's happening? Where's the next party? Let's have a good time. Let's get drunk; let's get high."

The fact that teens are full of energy does not have to be negative. It is a part of life. But if this energy is not channeled in the right direction, it can become negative and be very destructive. Kids have to be busy; therefore, parents must provide opportunities for them to keep busy doing the right things. Teens want and need positive alternatives into which they can channel their energy.

e) Teens often rebel against or question what exists.

Conflicts between teens and parents are almost inevitable when youth begin to question and challenge what exists. No institution is safe from the questions of youth.

School: "Why do I have to go to school?" "I don't believe this history stuff; they are trying to brainwash us."

Church: "How do I know God really exists?" "There are so many religions, which one is real?" "I don't believe this God stuff just because you do, Dad."

Politics: "All these politicians are just clowns; they're lying to us. They need to be tossed out." "Maybe this capitalist democracy stuff is wrong. Maybe communism is better."

Usually parents have already settled these issues for themselves. Since they went through the same thing some years ago so, they have no more questions. But this situation needs to be handled correctly also. As painful as it may be, parents and society as a whole need to answer a teenager's question honestly and not force their opinion on him or her. Let teens determine for themselves what truth is; you adults just provide the best information you can.

f) Teens take chances.

While parents settle the issues in their minds, young people blurt out their feelings and do things before thinking or weighing the consequences. Teens often experiment. They want to "go where no man has gone before" and check out "the final frontier." How many times do teens do things they later regret? Experiment with things their parents have already tried?

It is interesting to note that adults will speak to children about things they themselves have already been through, kids will listen and then go out and experiment with the very same thing. Over and over again I have talked to young people about my life on drugs and the time I spent on the street, yet they do the very same things. One high school student said to me, "You had your time; it's our time now." The sentiment he expressed was, "It's my time to experiment, to take some chances."

g) Teens have a respect for truth.

A song of years ago noted, "Everybody's searching for a hero, someone to look up to." Today's youth, like those before, are searching for someone to look up to. They don't like hypocrites; they are looking for adults who have enduring principles, whether they agree or disagree with those principles.

Believe it or not, kids cry out for discipline, direction and purpose. They look up to and respect adults who have strong moral convictions and who dare to care enough for those teens to not let them destroy themselves. Teens also look up to other teens whom they perceive to be strong in their convictions, who know the difference between wrong and right. Truth from the pages of the most important book in the world and from the lives of those who know it is something many youth cry out for.

h) Teens are great collaborators.

Peer pressure is a fact of teenage blues. Teenagers experience gratification from impressing each other, from beating "the system." Teens often plan together. If they intend to sneak off for the night or go to a party they are not supposed to attend, they plan to bear the consequences together or to beat the system together. Teens hardly ever do anything that is not designed to impress their peers. Parents are different. They do not usually collaborate when dealing with children, but children collaborate when dealing with parents.

What Is the Nature and Makeup of Parents?

a) Parents are wise.

Often parents have accumulated wisdom over the years. From their experiences, they know better. A television show that aired some years ago was titled "Father Knows Best." Many times parents already went through what their children go through and gained wisdom from the "school of hard knocks." Even your parents are wise because they experienced the things you have and lived to tell the story. They remember what they went through and know your story before you finish telling it.

b) Parents are realists.

A parent may say something like, "Son, you might as well get used to it; the world isn't going to change. I tried that before." Parents tend to think in realistic terms. They went through their own period of idealism and became resigned to what they consider the facts of life. They know certain things never or hardly ever change, so time is better spent on something else. Parents tend to view things realistically and base their judgments on what happened before.

c) Parents are practical.

Parents normally are inclined to calculate the risks and rewards and to determine what's most practical before making a decision. A young person often acts first and worries about consequences later. Parents do the opposite. They think first and proceed cautiously. If something appears uncertain or too risky, a parent will, in most cases, tell the teen who is ready to do it, not to proceed with it. Sometimes that is good. Other times that may actually rob a teen of an opportunity. Nevertheless, it is a part of parents' makeup.

d) Parents often are settled.

When parents were much younger, they did the same things their teens do. Many parents of today were activists, protesting about war, racism or injustice. As they grew older, such causes gave way to the realities of making ends meet and providing for their families. They don't feel like protesting any longer. They are comfortable in what they have already fought for and achieved. Therefore, parents are not very enthusiastic at the activism of teens.

e) Parents are protective.

Parents want to make sure their children don't get hurt or feel pain. They remember the mistakes they themselves made and try to prevent their children from making the same mistakes. Again that is sometimes positive, but it can become negative when parents are overprotective. Protection is, however, a fact of parental life. No matter how long we exist as human beings, parents will always tend to be protective or even overprotective.

f) Today's parents are busy.

Today's parents live at a pace that is unparalleled in the history of the human race. There is so much to do, but there never seems to be enough time in which to do it. Parents sometimes have two jobs, work late or are involved in something that prevents them from being available to their children. Often parents spend more time at work and on the road than they do at home. When dealing with the immediate issues of earning a living and of self-preservation, children are often an afterthought.

So How Do the Two Come Together?

It is a fact of life that, regardless of feelings or sentiments, parents outrank children. Every army has privates, generals, lieutenants, sergeants and so on. It just so happens that in the family structure, parents have been appointed generals by the Commander-in-Chief (God). That does not mean parents are always right or even right most of the times. It just means that that is the position they occupy. God works by authority and in order.

Children are commanded by the Commander-in-Chief to obey their parents. Of course, there is a phrase that says to obey them "in the Lord." Children can't always obey parents who are not "in the Lord." Children are to obey parents except in severe circumstance, where parents require children to act outside the law or when they abuse children. The Bible notes that parents should not provoke children, "Fathers, do not embitter your children, or they will become discouraged" (Colossians 3:21), or cause them to go against the established authority. We will deal with this subject a little more as we continue, but the general rule is, parents are higher in rank and even where there is a lack of respect for the person, the position must still be respected.

How Do Parents Earn the Respect of Their Children and Retain the Right of Their Position?

a) Parents are supposed to provide.

It is the responsibility of the parents to provide and make provisions for the children they bring into the world. Children do not ask to be born. Whenever children are brought into this world, the parent or parents have the responsibility of providing the necessities for their children, according to the parents' abilities. Note what the Bible says concerning this responsibility:

> ...After all, children should not have to save up for their parents, but parents for their children (2 Corinthians 12:14).

Parents should provide food, shelter and clothing, according to their abilities. Parents should not waste money by buying everything their children desire. Many times children lack discretion; they would buy anything they could. After all, they don't have to work. You should not have children if you are not prepared to provide for them.

b) Parents should not provoke children.

Parents should not abuse the authority God gave them by abusing their children, by failing to provide for them or by living a life of double standards. "Provoking children" could mean being too restrictive, abusive or unfair with expectations or living contrary to God's Word and still expecting children to obey without question. Note again what the Bible says:

> Fathers, do not exasperate your children; instead, bring them up in the training and instruction of the Lord (Ephesians 6:4).

Parents should remember that their teens are only a few years away from becoming parents also. Teenagers of today become the parents of tomorrow. Today's parents must ensure that their way of life does not drive their children in the wrong direction. Rather, their lifestyle should point young people to the path they would want to follow.

c) Parents should care for children.

There is a verse of scripture that states, "Children are a treasure from the Lord" (Psalms 127:3). However, in today's busy and mixed-up societies, children are seen more as a burden than as a treasure. Parents sometimes don't care about or for their children. Caring does not mean simply providing for their daily needs, it also means teaching them the Word and taking time to see that their concerns are looked after and their questions about life answered.

A parent who cares will spend time with his or her children and talk to them about what the children want to talk about. How many teens become distant from their parents because of one-way communication? Some parents only talk to their children when the children are in trouble or failed to carry out an assigned task. "Johnny, have you mowed the lawn like I asked you to?" "Susie, did you do the dishes as you were instructed?" It is important to talk to your children about things they want to dicuss. Ask teens about their favorite music group or favorite basketball team. The more you talk with them, the more you learn about teens. Parents must take good care of what God has entrusted to them.

d) Parents are supposed to discipline children.

This issue is a big one for both parents and teens. Teenagers know that discipline is a painful part of love and actually want to be disciplined. A parent who takes time to correct a young person may not be liked at that moment, but he or she will be respected. The Bible states very clearly that if you ignore discipline, your children will go astray. How many times have you seen a spoiled brat? Worse yet, a rich little spoiled brat?

Of course, when a child reaches those teen years, the method of discipline should change. Younger children often need physical discipline. However, if a child has been under your care for thirteen years and does not respond to your discipline, you did not discipline them properly during their earlier years and physical punishment is no longer the answer. The revocation of privileges, added chores, stricter curfews, restrictions on where he or she can go or reduced allowances can be used in disciplining a teen. Keep in mind that the discipline needs to be appropriate to the situation.

In administering discipline, however, parents should not enforce what has not been defined. Parents should communicate very clearly to teens what the ground rules and boundaries are and what the consequences will be for crossing those boundaries. Then, if the teen violates a rule that was already clearly defined, he or she has agreed that the only thing he or she can do is accept the punishment.

e) Parents must encourage.

Encouragement is a part of nurturing. Parents must be there for their children. You as a parent might take it lightly when you don't keep a promise, but teens don't. Let your word be good. Show up for the play they are in at school. Be at the ballgame when they play. If they make good grades, reward them. Even if they make mistakes, encourage them to try again and to do better.

If you have good children, don't frustrate them. I have seen parents whose children are well-behaved, ordinary kids, yet they treat their children as if they were the most rotten teens in the world. Thank God if you have a teen who keeps his or her word, doesn't do drugs and is not promiscuous. Give them more responsibility as they demonstrate their ability to be trusted. I have also known of parents who denied their children attendance at a church or youth group meeting as a punishment. Don't do that. Youth groups and church are the two places they are most likely to get spiritual food and counsel. There are many other things parents can deny children. Youth need responsibility in order to grow.

f) Parents need to listen and relate.

Another old saying that concerns young people is "Children should be seen and not heard." That is wrong.

Children need a forum to be heard. If you don't provide them with a forum where they can be heard, there are many other people who will, and they don't have your heart and don't care about your children. Parents must understand what motivates their children, what interests them, what music they listen to, which books they read and who they consider their heroes.

Parents who don't know what music their children listen to are out of touch. Today's musicians and entertainers tell teens to get high, kill, steal, rape and rebel. Don't believe just me; stop by your nearest music store and read the lyrics.

If you know what music your children listen to, you have a better idea of where their heads are. You might not be able to be a teen again, but you must learn to relate. Ask your teens questions like, "What are some of the new sayings? What do they mean?" Often theirs is a different world, one to which parents don't have ready access. Parents must listen and relate or they could lose touch with their children and just call it a generation gap. A parent's world is obvious to teens, but a teen's world is not obvious to parents. Parents may assume a lot and yet know very little.

g) Parents must communicate.

There is no excuse for not communicating. I don't mean just communication, I mean two-way communication. Every parent-teen relationship needs a forum for resolving conflicts. Also, parents should learn to say "We're sorry" when they are wrong and to forgive when necessary. Forgiveness gets rid of bitterness.

Parents must also remember to keep problems at home or between themselves and a counselor. Parents' friends do not need to know what is happening between the parents and their children. Young people do not want to hear about how their parents talk about them to other parents. Teens may then communicate with parents even less than before.

Parents must take the idealism of youth and help it merge with realism. Youth ask many questions, and parents need to help find the answers. Parents don't need to tell teens to not ask the questions. Punishment is not an appropriate way for parents to escape their parental responsibility of face-to-face communication.

h) Parents must prepare teenagers to leave home.

Believe it or not, children are only supposed to be with parents for a time. Children are born to leave. A parent's job is to prepare his or her children to leave home. The best parents are the ones whose children are well prepared to live outside the confines of their home.

As teens grow, they should progressively be given more responsibility and encouraged to start their own lives by planning for the future. The worst thing is for a young person who is "Mamma's boy" or "Daddy's girl" to get married expecting what he or she left behind at the parents' home and, when he or she doesn't get it, run back home to Daddy or Mommy. Parents should not smother young people or prepare them to stay in the house forever. Parents need to learn to commit their children to God. Once parents have done what they should, there is nothing left to do. Parents must exercise wisdom but remember to let the children go after doing their best.

What Is a Teen Supposed to Do?

a) Teens should obey "in the Lord."

As I noted earlier, parents outrank children. Parents have a higher position in the army. According to God's law, a teenager is a "private" and in some cases just a "recruit." You teens must recognize your parents' position and respect it.

Your parents are not always right, but they are in charge and unless they grossly violate the rules of the game, you have no right to overturn or rebel against their decisions.

There should be discussion, your point of view should be known, but the final say belongs to the generals commissioned by the Commander-in-Chief. The scripture that follows shows us how God feels about parental instruction.

Listen, my son, to your father's instruction and do not forsake your mother's teaching. They will be a garland to grace your head and a chain to adorn your neck (Proverbs 1:8-9).

Listen to your parents' instruction unless it is obviously out of line with God's Word. You cannot really be expected to obey a parent who asks you to take drugs or to rob a bank. But you are expected to obey a parent who gives you reasonable instructions in a spirit of love and fairness. Pray for your parents and do your best to help them understand your point of view, but unless they blatantly go against God, you should obey.

b) Teens must respect parents.

The Bible issues a very clear command that has a blessing attached to it. The command is to honor your father and mother.

> "Honor your father and mother"—which is the first commandment with a promise—"that it may go well with you and that you may enjoy long life on the earth" (Ephesians 6:2-3).

In other words, respect them. Your parents are your caretakers in this world until you are old enough and wise enough to make it on your own. Until that time, and even after you leave home, you should always respect and honor your parents. It is important to not be disrespectful or ashamed of your parents. This is the one command from God that indicates He is not pleased if you are disrespectful. In fact, this command indicates that your life may be shortened if you fail to respect your parents. If you dishonor your parents, God will dishonor you. He said so.

c) Teens should deserve responsibility.

Don't ask for more responsibility until you act correctly with what you already have. If your parents give you a curfew and you agree to be home at 11:00 P.M., when you come home with that flat tire story at 1:00 A.M., they should not even let you out the house during daylight. So if you want more responsibility, live up to your part of the bargain. You should keep your word so well that they can't help but see how responsible you are and increase the amount of freedom you have. If you will be late for a legitimate reason, make sure you call. Don't make your parents worry because of the dumb things you do. Parents are proud of responsible children.

If you are supposed to go to the school party, don't sneak off with Donna and lie about it. The more you cheat and lie, the less responsibility you deserve. If you choose not to be responsible, your parents are supposed to discipline you. This scripture in the Book of Proverbs shows the role discipline plays in the mind of the Lord and of parents.

My son, do not despise the Lord's discipline and do not resent his rebuke, because the Lord disciplines those he loves, as a father the son he delights in (Proverbs 3:11-12).

A good parent disciplines in love because he or she wants the son or daughter to be responsible. A bad parent disciplines abusively. But if you are irresponsible, your parents will have to discipline you.

d) Teens need to pray for parents.

Parents should listen to and understand teens, but it is one of the realities of life today that they often don't. Many times when I talk to teens they say, "Talk to my parents? Are you kidding? I have tried and tried but they won't listen or appreciate my point of view." Because that is so often true, children sometimes have to appeal to the Commander-in-Chief and say, "Chief, You are in charge of this situation. Help my parents understand and communicate with me."

You may be surprised at what good can be done and what can be accomplished if you pray regularly for your parents. Parents are not enemies. You can do all you know to do and talk to parents, but if a parent is obnoxious and unwilling to cooperate, you can only pray and continue to do your best despite the circumstances. Be as helpful and as cooperative as you can, and don't be the one to cause further problems or to aggravate the situation. Give your parents a reason so they can understand you better. Show them that you know how to love. Let them see Jesus in you.

e) Teens should report a parent who is grossly out of order.

If your parents abuse you physically or sexually, you have gone beyond the stage where you obey "in the Lord." Perhaps for your own physical and mental survival you need to report your parents to the appropriate authorities and get out of the situation until some resolution can be made. Sometimes things happen in step-parent or other nontraditional family units that result in your need to get out of a situation quickly. In fact, problems can develop even in normal or traditional family units that require your taking action for your own protection. But before you do so, consult your youth pastor, guidance counselor or another adult in whom you have confidence.

All authorities and power are ultimately subject to God. If parents are grossly violating God's law, there are some people with appropriate "authority" to deal with them. The Book of Romans deals very clearly with this topic. These verses show that we all—parents, teens, citizens, governments—are responsible to a higher authority.

> Everyone must submit himself to the governing authorities, for there is no authority except that which God has established. The authorities that exist have been established by God. Consequently, he who rebels against the authority is rebelling against what God has instituted, and those who do so will bring judgment on themselves. For rulers hold no terror for those who do right, but for those who do wrong. Do you want to be free from fear of the one in authority? Then do what is right and he will commend you. For he is God's servant to do you good. But if you do wrong, be afraid, for he does not bear the sword for nothing... (Romans 13:1-4).

f) Some teens have no parents.

In the world which we live in today, some children actually grow up on their own. A parent may be there, but may not provide or fulfill any of the parental functions. Some teens have to grow themselves up and look to others who are not their parents, for direction, guidance and counsel. It is important to talk to someone and to be able to get help when you need it or to get advice in making decisions. In some cases you could talk to a school guidance counselor, a youth pastor, a pastor, a Christian friend or an adult in whom you have confidence.

Some of you must be strong on your own and some of you must be parents to your parents. Many times, through your godly living and example, you teach your parents how to live and how to be responsible. God will help you as you continue to serve Him and place Him first in your life. No matter how difficult the situation is, "hold fast" to the things you have learned in the Word and let God do the rest.

Points to Remember

For Teens

Parents Are: Wise, Settled, Busy, Practical, Protective, Realists.

1. Teens should deserve responsibility.

2. If you dishonor your parents, God will dishonor you.

3. Parents are not always right, but they are in charge and unless they grossly violate the rules of the game, you have no right to overturn or rebel against their decisions.

4. You need to pray for your parents.

For Parents

Teens Are: Idealistic, Energetic, Chance Takers, Identity Seekers, Collaborators, Truth Seekers, Sometimes Rebellious, Living in Their Own Language and Culture.

1. Prepare teenagers to leave home.

2. Communicate; but don't use one-way communication, use two-way communication.

3. Parents need to listen and relate.

4. Parents must encourage.

5. Parent are supposed to discipline children.

6. Parents should care for children.

7. Parents should not provoke children.

3 | Sex, Love & Relationships

I saw her just the other day
and I knew I was in Love,
The way she walked,
the way she talked,
I could not resist,
I knew it would be bliss,
How could I Miss with this sis

(Davy B)

Let's Talk about Sex

In speaking of things as out of order, that is no more evident than in attitudes toward sex and relationships. Even in church circles the question may arise, "Why would we talk about sex to young church people?" The fact is, the church is not a refuge from sexual issues, no matter what age group.

If we don't tell you the truth, then you will learn what you need to know about sex from the wrong sources.

One of the silliest notions in the world is that Christians shouldn't talk about sex. We ought to know more about the real purpose of sex than anyone one else because we know the Maker and Inventor of sex.

Believe me, as Christians we must talk about sex. Teens live in a real world, full of pressure, advertising sex 27 hours a day during the week and 3 times on Sunday. Teens live in a world which doesn't know the purpose of sex and where the abuse of sex is prevalent. If you don't believe me, a young person I know actually asked the question, "Since it's wrong to have sex, is God against oral sex?" He was a Christian young person. We had better talk about sex.

Wrong Sex

Sex used outside of its purpose is responsible for more problems in the world today than any other single factor. Think of it. Every time sex outside of marriage is practiced, one of the following results: a broken home, an unwanted pregnancy, an abortion, a child without a father, social deviance, overpopulation, welfare, a damaged teen, AIDS, death and destruction.

You live in a world where teenage sex is accepted as fact, even encouraged directly and indirectly. In fact many, many parents, teachers and others don't see anything wrong with teenage sex. Some cable and satellite owners can get XXX rated movies which their children often watch unabated. Sex is everywhere and in just about everything the world does today. Teens have access to sex: sex on television, sex in music, sex in the church, sex in the newspaper, sex in the magazines; sex everywhere and every day outside of God's original design for it. Often teenagers are not discouraged from having sex, they are just encouraged to wear a condom.

Telling a teenager to wear a condom is like telling a child to be careful with a hand grenade. They might be careful, but the mere nature of youth suggests that it is not something they need to deal with right now.

Actually, if you are a Christian, the question of "whether or not" is really not an issue. The Bible is very clear on sex. I can never understand why Christians debate whether or not homosexuality is wrong or if fornication is wrong. If you read the Book and are a complete idiot, you still could not have any problem in determining what is right and wrong. God was never ambivalent about sex. He invented it and wrote the book on how it should be used.

And live a life of love, just as Christ loved us and gave himself up for us as a fragrant offering and sacrifice to God. But among you there must not be even a hint of sexual immorality, or any kind of impurity... (Ephesians 5:2-3).

To call yourself a Christian and suggest that God said something different because "times have changed" is pretty stupid. I cannot understand how anyone can read the Bible and still say that God suggested sex outside of marriage was subject to conditions in the world or to changing times. That is just not so. Actually, if we try to change the Bible like that, we should not even call a Sunday morning service "church" anymore. We should maybe call it "today's gathering of conventional wisdom where we worship the god we created to satisfy our own appetites." If you want to create your own religion and your own god, you should write your own book and make your own heaven. Jehovah is just not into changing His mind to please a mixed-up generation.

There is no such thing as safe sex unless you abide by its design in the mind of the Maker. If, as a young person, you choose to go another way, then the issue becomes one of "what is the safest" rather than "what is safe." Nothing is "safe" when it comes to sex. Many of the children in the world today were born to someone who wore a condom. Many people in the world today who have AIDS and other venereal diseases wore condoms. It is foolish to think that there is anything called "safe sex" for a teen. Birth control and other subjects for the sexually active teen are really not in God's plan, although people in this mixed-up world who chose to walk the wrong road need to be advised of the best and worst alternatives of their choice. That leads me to my most important question about sex.

Who Invented Sex?

The way sex is so often abused and misused today, some people would say *Playboy* or *Penthouse* invented sex. Some might say the guys on the blocks. Some might say a popular rock star or a rap artist. But if you answered none of the above, you were right. *Guess who invented sex? GOD. That's right, GOD invented sex.*

Some of those people want you to think they personally invented sex, but God came up with the idea Himself. God, when He designed men and women, designed sex and planned how it would operate to achieve the maximum benefit. Now if I had a choice between taking instructions from the manufacturer and the user, I would have to choose the manufacturer.

The world tries to tell you that all teens are having sex, but that is obviously not true. Many do not and will not because they choose to listen to God and not to man. One of satan's most devious plots is to make young people feel guilty because they have not had sex. Thousands and millions of young people have made the right choice and kept silent because of fear and peer pressure.

After God designed sex, He wrote the manual on how to use it. What does the manual say? It says, "Use only in marriage."

Flee from sexual immorality. All other sins a man commits are outside his body, but he who sins sexually sins against his own body. Do you not know that your body is a temple of the Holy Spirit, who is in you, whom you have received from God? You are not you own; you were bought at a price. Therefore honor God with your body (1 Corinthians 6:18-20).

That is God's instruction to you. He also has said that sex is designed for marriage. If God said He designed it for a particular purpose, then it stands to reason we should use it only for that purpose. God has also said that we should run away (flee) from fornication because He knew that sex outside of marriage would only cause frustration and heartache. How many young people have engaged in sex, only to regret it for years to come due to an unwanted pregnancy, sex-related diseases or other psychological problems?

One of the saddest statistics often quoted today is that teenagers are the largest and fastest growing group of AIDS infected persons.

It is always easier on your conscience and more beneficial to do things God's way. Pre-marital sex just builds a sexual appetite that can be satisfied only by more sex...and more and more!

Relationships

In order to properly understand sex and how it should be practiced, we must look at relationships first. Of course, we live in a world where the pressure to have sex outside of marriage is almost overwhelming for all teens, including the ones who carry Bibles and say, "Praise the Lord." Actually, sex should not even be thought of outside a long-term, honest and committed (marriage) relationship. But we do live in a real and powerfully influential world, so we must look at what teens can do to properly handle the day-to-day pressures that concern sexual issues.

It is much better, and you end up in much happier relationships, if you live the right way. In my own life I came to realize, after spending most of my time disobeying God, that we are always happier when we do things the right way. Most of my discussion of sex here concerns the way to build proper relationships. It will also include some guidelines that can help you understand the boundaries you should consider in a relationship.

Stages of Relationships

They Meet: Acquaintances...

I saw her just the other day
and I knew I was in Love,
The way she walked,
the way she talked,
I could not resist,
I Knew it would be bliss,
How could I Miss with this sis

That sounds wonderful and so romantic, but it is so un-true. *You can't really love someone you don't know*. What is expressed here is simply attraction: "I like what I see." That is not love. Too many people confuse attraction with love and passion with substance. Relationships function on different levels and each level has its own rules. If you see someone for the first time, or if you cross paths from day to day but never really talk much, that person is just an acquaintance, someone you met.

It just does not make sense to hop into bed with someone you don't know. Would you open your bank account to someone you met yesterday?

No, you wouldn't open your bank account because it takes time to establish that level of trust. An acquaintance is someone with whom you have occasional contact. You may talk about the weather or ask general questions that relate to public information. You may talk about school, your favorite food, sports or whatever general subject may arise. You don't fall in love with acquaintances because, contrary to popular opinion, love is a conscious decision based upon the vital information you discover about a person.

Many teenagers see a pretty girl and decide "this is love" when it really isn't love at all. Let's say the girl's name is Toni, and she's so fine she could blow your mind. You think you're in love and you tell all your friends, "This is it; I'm in love." Later on, after you really get to know her, you find that she's conceited, stuck up, does not really care about you and in fact, only tolerates you because her friends thought you were cute. Are you still in love when you find out the truth? Well no, because the truth is, you were never in love in the first place. Love may be influenced by attraction, but attraction does not mean love.

Actually, the most constructive activity for teens is talking. Meeting someone for the first time or seeing someone every now and then is just an opportunity for you to get to know the person and see if you really like him or her. Then you decide if the relationship should progress beyond the level of acquaintance. Actually, you should view each acquaintance as an opportunity for you to share the love of God, with no strings attached. Acquaintances may be Christian or non-Christian. It is important to have non-Christian acquaintances so you can witness to them and possibly help them or direct them to the Lord. You never hop into bed or discuss your intimate life with an acquaintance.

For most teens, the most important thing to do is to learn to relate to the opposite sex: how to treat a lady right or how to act in the presence of a young man. If you are sixteen-years-old, don't burden yourself with the complexities of commitment because there is so much you need to learn. You've got school, and you've a career out there in the future. So don't get too serious and tie yourself into a relationship that probably will last only until you both become a little older and wiser.

Sex is a gift from God given to consummate legal union of two people. This gift should only be given in a marriage relationship, to the person that you love, trust, respect and said "I do" to. You cannot give the same gift over and over again to several persons. Otherwise the gift will have little value and eventually be ready for the trash bin. Remember, most teens "fall in love" at least four or five times between the ninth grade and their second year of college.

They Greet: Casual...

After you have gotten to know someone as an acquaintance and found out that you have much in common, the next level of relationship is casual. "Casual" indicates that this person is someone you know, the two of you share some common interests, activities and concerns. You go a little deeper in conversation, although topics are still of a general nature, dealing with opinions, ideas, wishes and goals.

As you talk to each other, you learn about each other—the positive and the negative qualities. In a casual relationship, you can point out to a person things you notice and learn to identify negative and positive qualities in each other. Talking to each other and learning more about your "friend" will help you determine whether you really like the person and how you like them. One of the first things you should talk about is the person's spiritual life—where is he or she at?

Never go anywhere beyond the acquaintance level in a relationship if you have questions about a person's spiritual direction.

If you are a Christian and your "friend" is not, it is better if you do not go any deeper in a relationship, because the mix never works. If you were searching for a formula for disaster, you couldn't find a better one than light and darkness walking together. The Bible asks how two could walk together if they don't agree and how light could fellowship with darkness.

Do not be yoked together with unbelievers. For what do righteousness and wickedness have in common? Or what fellowship can light have with darkness? (2 Corinthians 6:14).

The Bible is so clear on this issue, yet we often try to figure out how to get around what God says because he or she is "so cute." It just doesn't work.

After interacting and talking, you may decide it's best for this relationship to remain on the acquaintance level because the two of you are not going in the same or in compatible directions in life. Of course, if someone is a casual friend of the opposite sex, it means you may talk to each other on the phone and meet in public places. If you do go out, it is normally with others and there is no physical contact in this type of relationship. That does not mean elaborate dinners or expensive dates or gifts. If someone is a casual friend, you don't go out and buy an $800 ring with the money you earned working at McDonalds or with your allowance that you saved for six years.

In any relationship, both persons should be clear on where the other stands. Too many times I've seen relationships where a young guy is madly "in love" with a young lady and as far as she is concerned, he is just a "friend." She doesn't know what he is thinking but he thinks she is thinking the way he is. Then one day she is seen walking to class with "another guy." Homeboy then becomes blue in the face, approaches the young lady and wants her to explain. She says, "I thought we were just friends." Of course he is shattered. He *thought* he was in love.

Clear communication is so vital to relationships. Remember, in a casual relationship you exchange ideas and wishes and note positive qualities in each other. You get to know more about the person: their family background, their friends, who they hang out with, what kind of music they listen to, what kind of parties they like to attend. If they hang out with wild or drug-oriented friends, that should say something to you. It is important because casual friends can become close friends. You would not want to become close to someone only to find out that the two of you were headed in different directions. That can cause tension and can lead to unnecessary conflicts.

In light of todays world and the pressure of society towards young people and sex, perhaps there should be no physical contact in a casual relationship. You certainly should not lock the door of your bedroom and having a deep conversation with no words. The teenage tradition of "making out" in the back seat of a car or elsewhere is an invitation to problems. Leading a thirsty man to the water is dangerous; he will want to drink. You should not be in private situations with a casual friend. You should not be in your bedroom. You should not be home or anywhere private alone together. No one is strong enough, and even if you are, it is foolish to play with fire.

Teenagers are not ready for sex because the Maker said so. Whenever you contemplate sex, you should also contemplate having a family, paying bills and being on your own, because these and sex are meant to go together. I know we live in a world where sexual pressure is everywhere. I know teenage hormones are stimulated by an environment that encourages sexual activity. But the truth is, we cannot argue with God. If He very clearly said to do something a certain way, then it is always better to do it His way. Countless teens who dropped out of school, got married prematurely or had abortions can testify that it is better to do it by the Book.

So remember that the main activity you should engage in is talking. It is important to talk. Talking provides both parties with information and helps them avoid wrong assumptions. *Learn to make friends, not lovers.* If you start out a relationship by being "in love," then your heart will be "broken" when you discover that you started at the wrong place. You both assumed wrong and at least one person has to deal with an unneccessary emotional hurt. Don't start looking for rings and dresses after the first date!

In addition to talking, you should pray for one another. You may also pray together, but avoid praying together in private settings. (How many prayer sessions have turned into less than holy and constructive activities?)

In this type of relationship, you should not be looking for a return on your investment. Some guys and girls work hard to win the affection of a special person. They spend all their money on that person and then they expect a big payday. There should not be any strings attached to a date. Have fun and please don't be too serious; your teen years are some of the best you will have in life. Don't waste these wonderful years by getting too serious. I believe it is important to have more than one friend, for both guys and gals. Having several friends of the opposite sex gives you a better picture of what men or women are all about. Then you can compare personalities and interests to help you later decide what type of marriage partner you would wish to have.

Double Dates...

It is important for casual friends to go on double dates or in groups to avoid easy attachment. It also protects you from society and in some cases from the church people who try to "match" couples and start hollering marriage the first time they see you with someone.

In a casual friendship, one should not be concerned about the physical appearance of a friend. So often we damage opportunities to meet and get to know wonderful people by deciding on a criteria of good looks without considering character and beauty beyond the skin-deep kind. Being good-looking, cute or fine does not make a person good. If you get hung up on looks, it could stop you from seeing the real person on the inside. Remember, many pretty girls or handsome guys have no character.

Above all, learn to relate. You may find out things about people you never knew. You may cause someone to bring out treasures even they did not know they possessed simply by being a friend and talking to them.

It Gets Sweet *Close*.

> **I no longer call you servants, because a servant does not know his master's business. Instead, I have called you friends, for everything that I learned from my Father I have made known to you** (John 15:15).

The next level beyond casual friendship is that of close friendship. A person cannot become close to you overnight. As Jesus noted in the scripture just quoted, a friend knows the "business" of his or her friend. An old song of years ago stated, "Take time to know her, it's not an overnight thing." It takes months of conversation and interaction to really get to know a person.

Most teens should remain in acquaintance and casual relationships only. When a real close relationship develops, it has started down the road to marriage. It is not good to be on the road to marriage and not be old enough, strong enough or mature enough to deal with it. You think you have problems now, just wait until you have to change diapers in the middle of the night or pay bills every month. Take your time, young people, a lot of living is ahead.

A close relationship should be based on mutual life goals. You should know that you are headed in the same direction as the person to whom you are close, especially if the person is of the opposite sex. Closeness brings familiarity and familiarity brings comfort. It is easy to let your guard down with someone you know well. So if you see yourself heading in that direction, take a good look at the person and decide if you are on the same wavelength spiritually, mentally and otherwise.

Some relationships between a guy who wants to be a doctor and a girl who wants to be a janitress do work, but it is very unlikely. The same holds true for a guy who is serious about his relationship with the Lord and about his future and the girl who is religious, but not serious about her relationship with the Lord. The closer you become, the more freedom you should have to suggest and discuss things about each other that will help you reach your individual life goals. Learn to assist the other person in fulfilling his or her dreams and aspirations. The focus of a close friendship is to develop character.

You should not have several close relationships with persons of the opposite sex. It is much too emotionally demanding to be close to more than one person of the opposite sex. Someone will be cheated and then there will be conflict because it is just not right.

Once you develop a close relationship, you should explore that relationship and decide whether you will continue or whether you need to ask this person to return to a casual relationship before you get into another close relationship. You need to set standards when it comes to the opposite sex. Early in your teen life you should set standards as to what is right and wrong and what you will and will not do. Draw the line for yourself using God, His Word and your conscience as your guide.

Even though you may be close to someone of the opposite sex, you should not allow them to touch you under your clothes or engage in any activity that precipitates sex. Necking, heavy petting or other type of sexual arousal is a ticket to frustration and pain. Again, because of the way sex is exploited and the realistic fact that many Christian teenagers compromise Biblical standards, the best rule to sex is no physical contact. However, each person, especially females, must set rules that do not compromise his or her stand as a Christian.

One of the facts of life is that girls must be more careful and more forceful since they stand to lose so much more and because guys are, or at least used to be, the aggressors sexually. As some Christians would say, no "body ministry" in the back seat of a car or undressing your date and touching intimate body parts. Let your standards be known by your girlfriend or boyfriend. If he or she doesn't respect the standards you set, then you know your friend is not really a friend. It's time to move on and sever any relationship where someone doesn't respect your standards or tries to get you to do something for his or her personal gratification. In most cases teens don't know enough about the opposite sex to realize what he or she is thinking. A lady wants to be treated like a lady, but ladies often don't understand that men naturally want to satisfy their immediate urges as opposed to being romantic. That is a fact of life that destroys so many teen girls. They are thinking love and guys are thinking sex.

At this point in a close relationship, you should know a lot about each other: your dreams, hopes, career aspirations and goals for the future. Both of you should have similar types of friends. I must repeat that, at this stage, you should not have a close friend of the same or of the opposite sex who is not a Christian because you reveal things to close friends. You confide in such a person and, as you confide in each other, defenses break down and so on. Darkness does not do a very good job of advising light. For example, an unsaved girl might advise you, a Christian girl, to get back at your boyfriend by going out with someone else. Nonbelievers do not have godly solutions to problems, and if you want to win in life, listening to advice that is not based upon God's Word will certainly not help you do that.

As in every other stage of relationship, talking should be the main activity. Physical contact should be limited and placed behind spiritual and mental stimulation. God should be the center of your relationship. You should never go to your friend's apartment, travel together alone or put yourself in compromising situations. The spirit is willing, but the flesh is weak.

> ...each of you should learn to control his own body in a way that is holy and honorable, not in passionate lust like the heathen, who do not know God (1 Thessalonians 4:4-5).

> For those who sleep, sleep at night, and those who get drunk, get drunk at night. But since we belong to the day, let us be self-controlled... (1 Thessalonians 5:7-8).

Keeping control over your body is much harder than you think. Talking, praying, playing, studying and exercising are important ways of communication. The less you talk, the more you get into mattress polo and bedtimes stories. Remember, petting only teaches you more than you need to know about the strength of hormones.

When I dated my wife, we really grew and got to know each other by reading the Bible together, sharing things from the Word that built each other up and listening to tapes. We had fun going to restaurants, riding motorbikes and just taking in the simple pleasures of life. Make sure you learn to laugh with and at each other; have fun in your relationships. Seriousness is for adults who are over the hill, like your parents (smile).

Time to Be Complete: Intimate

If you have had a close friend (boyfriend or girlfriend) for a long period of time (at least six months; the younger you are, the longer the period should be), you have to begin thinking about marriage. However, it is not good to get into a serious or close relationship too early in life; it robs you of important knowledge you need to gain about the opposite sex. I have seen it happen over and over again.

For example, Johnny fell in love with Susie when they were sixteen. She was the apple of his eye; he could do no wrong in hers. They swore that this love would last forever; they would get married, raise a family together and no one would come between them. They walked to school together; he was by her house every night. They could not stop calling each other. It was love.

Then one day Susie went off to college and Johnny worked, making good money. He wrote her long love letters and sent her money. They were in love. She wrote back and made promises until she began to notice some things. She noticed that there were some mighty fine guys on campus. Some were even saved and had great aspirations for their lives. She began to think, "The only guy I ever went out with was Johnny, and I do love him, but I never really had a chance to find out what other guys were like." So she casually begins talking to Mike, who is not only cool, he is also going places. She still loves Johnny, but Mike makes her think of what life might be like. The more she talks to Mike, the more she realizes that they are more suited for each other. One day Johnny calls and says, "Where were you last night? I called and they said you were out with friends." Susie then begins to say..."Dear Johnny." Johnny is devastated.

That is another reason for taking your time and not tying yourself down too early in life.

Intimacy

This stage of relationship is the intimate stage. This level is based on commitment, long-term commitment, and follows the close stage. At this stage, the intimate stage, you should be working on each other's character and planning engagement or marriage. You should not be intimate with anyone you don't plan to marry. I'm not talking about just physical intimacy. You don't reveal important things about yourself to someone who is not very close to you. Exchanging private information is one of the most intimate elements in a relationship. It takes a long time and a long period of trusting before you can really talk to someone, especially someone of the opposite sex, about intimate things in your life.

The closer you grow in a relationship, the more freedom you should feel to advise, suggest and correct each other. Very often it is difficult to see your own faults and even when you do see your faults, it is difficult for you to admit them and take corrective action. That is where you can assist each other by honestly pointing out things that will lead to further character development. At this stage, commitment should be absolutely genuine, for you both would be vulnerable to the other.

Here is an interesting statistic: *God told us 28 times in the New Testament to flee fornication.* He said that basically because fornication is enticing, especially as you approach marriage. In fact, the closer you get to marriage, the more likely you are to fool yourself into thinking it wouldn't really be fornication because you're getting married anyway. For your own sake, resist the temptation and run away from it.

The standards you set for physical contact will be tested more at this stage than at any other. It is still important, however, to maintain your standards. If you find it extremely difficult to do so, do not prolong your engagement. In First Corinthians Paul tells us it is better to marry if you find yourself behaving in a way that is not right (7:9). Make doubly sure you are headed in the same directions and have compatible interests and educational goals. Do not forget, however, that the most important activity you can engage in at this stage is still talking.

"Love" will now be in full bloom. There may be candlelight dinners, gifts, flowers and various expressions of gratitude and love. It is especially important to avoid private meetings, being alone in each other's home and putting yourself in compromising situations. You already know enough about each other to know whether this person will make a good marriage partner. Don't complicate the situation by having to go down the aisle prematurely because you couldn't wait. I don't know how many cases I have seen in recent times where good Christian couples just couldn't or wouldn't wait. They ended up lessening the enjoyment of their first year of marriage by dealing with raising a child. The first year of marriage is important for getting to know each other in a new environment. There are many things that are better worked out if no children are present.

Spiritual intimacy is another element of this stage. If God is the center of your relationship, then spiritual intimacy is and should be your foremost objective. Build each other up in faith and in the practical aspects of each other's Christian walk. Work toward agreement and understanding. You should be able to share your deepest thoughts and convictions with this person. You should be refining one another, helping to point out character defects and causing one another to grow.

It is important to learn how to forgive and to discuss differences without angry arguments. The closer you get to marriage, the more you need to know about how to resolve conflicts. Conflicts of one kind or another are inevitable. Learn how to discuss and not argue, to forgive first and not wait on the other person to say "I'm sorry." You must stand by your principles and convictions in order to ensure meaningful and lasting quality relationships. *If you don't stand for something, you will fall for anything...it is a fact of life.*

Points to Remember

1. You can't really love someone you don't know.

2. Love is a decision based upon information, understanding and attraction.

3. *God* invented sex.

4. Christians should talk about sex.

5. Christians ought to know more about the real purpose of sex than anyone else, because we know the Maker and Inventor of sex.

6. Each person must set rules that do not compromise his or her stand as a Christian.

7. The boundaries you set should be based upon God's Word and your own conscience.

8. Never go anywhere in a relationship beyond the acquaintance level if you have questions about a person's spiritual direction.

9. Let your boyfriend or girlfriend know your standards. If he or she doesn't respect the standards you set, then you know your friend is not really a friend.

10. You should not have a close friend of the same or opposite sex who is not a Christian because you reveal things to close friends and confide in such persons.

11. It is especially important to avoid private meetings, being alone in each other's home and putting yourself in compromising situations.

12. The closer you get to marriage, the more likely you are to fool yourself into thinking having sex wouldn't really be fornication because you're getting married anyway.

13. You should not be intimate with anyone you don't plan to marry.

14. The less you talk, the more you get into mattress polo and bedtime stories.

4 They Go for the Fun...(Music, Movies and Entertainment)

This is the 20th century.
Any gun can play,
any fool can say
or do what he wants.
Society has no rules
so all we see are fools.

(Davy B)

Teens Want Fun

When talking about issues that face teens, we cannot possibly overlook the items listed in the title of this chapter. *Let's face it, kids just want to have fun* (like the song of some years ago, "Girls Just Want to Have Fun"). There is an element in every teen that is attracted to fun. Serious philosophy, great works of art and other complexities of life mean very little to a teenager. They want to have fun and are attracted to fun things. What are fun things to kids? Music, parties, movies and sports.

The world is full of entertainment for kids. Most kids, especially if they are Christians, are faced with an ever-growing difficulty in deciding what is good fun and what is bad fun. One of the sad realities of life today is what often seems innocent and fun often is not. Satan has somehow permeated every form of entertainment with his influence. Music is sometimes full of sexual deviance, movies are perverted, dance is dangerous and culture is criminal rather than creative. How often have you heard stories lately of where some heavy metal musician encouraged some young person to commit suicide or to worship the devil, or of movies so gory, ghastly and violent that they permanently damaged the faculties of some young person. One of the most bizarre things I have heard of lately is trading cards (like baseball cards) of serial killers.

Entertainment today often means watching someone brutally murdered or having sex (or deviant sex), listening to bizarre messages in music or watching dancers and rappers who might as well be having sex on stage. Against this backdrop, what is a Christian young person to do for entertainment and fun? Teens want to have fun, no matter what their educational, social or religious background might be. How do you make the right choices when it comes to having fun?

God's Jams (Music)

Let's take music for an example. The question that the normal Christian teen will ask is *"What's wrong with listening to the music of the day?"* *That is a very good question and one the ordinary church often just dismisses by the answer, "If you are a Christian, you wouldn't want to listen to anything that is not Christian." Some churches would say, "Listen to what you want to listen, as long as you come to church and pay your tithes." The truth is, there is a right and wrong way to every-thing. How you handle the question of music can, in many cases, mean the difference between life and death both physi-cally and spiritually.*

Some of today's music kills and some of it can lead a young person down the paths of unrighteousness. "I Want to Sex You Up" is not likely to lead you to a right relationship with God.

I still haven't answered your question though, of what you should do about music. Paul in the Bible said certain things that were direct from God and other things that were by inspiration. My thoughts on this subject are based upon my experience as a Christian and as a worker with teens.

Music Is a Tool

The first thing to be understood about music is that *music is a tool*. It is very difficult to call a certain type of music "bad" music. It is equally as difficult to call a certain type of music "Christian" music. What style of music is played in Heaven? What type of music does God like? Is God funky? Is He classical? Is He into heavy metal? When there is a jam session in Heaven, what do they play? Many times when people talk about church music they talk about their preference for a given style of music. People in the southern USA like their gospel music with a country flair. People in black communities like their "gospel" with a fast, hand clapping beat featuring organs and drums. The young man in Africa may like his "gospel" music to the sound of Conga drums. So what type of music is "God's"?

**God does not have a type of music that
He placed upon His Body and said,
"Play this only." Christian music is
more what you say than what you play.**

The content of the music, the lifestyle of the musician and his or her personal Christian commitment tells you whether or not the music is Christian. God is not, from what I can determine, interested in people's tastes. He is interested in reaching them on their level. If 99 percent of the world is listening to rap music, should we close our eyes and say, "God is not into rap"? If God used the jawbone of an ass to get the job done, should we tell Him what to use next? No. Let's not worship or argue about tools.

Some people worship a certain style of music that others argue whether or not is right. That is generally a waste of valuable time. Normal "church" or "Christian" music is unlikely to inspire the average teenager. Young people often want an alternative to what they already are into or like. If you like dance or rap music, let's make sure it has the right message.

If you check the Bible, God likes horns, drums, harps, cymbals, stringed instruments (guitars), clapping hands; just about everything you can think of. It is interesting to note that He seemed to like "loud" music because He told the musicians to play loudly. He also liked skillful music:

Praise the Lord with the harp; make music to him on the ten-stringed lyre. Sing to him a new song; play skillfully, and shout for joy (Psalms 33:2-3).

In Second Chronicles 5:11-14, God had a mean horn section. They played loud and long and then God came in and His glory filled the place. The truth is, God likes what you like. He created us to dominate. He agrees with what we name the animals or the music we decide to play as long as it is done unto Him. We have tried to fit God into our fashions and culture rather than to fit our fashions and culture into God's plan. God is too big to fit into a single culture, style or fashion. These things are so trivial to God that not one verse of scripture tells us anything about a style of music that God likes. The Bible talks about there being weightier matters of the law.

Who to and Who Not to Listen to

You should listen to music that points to God and that builds up your personal relationship with Him. "Let's have sex tonight" does not build you up or convey what the Bible says, so you should not listen to it. Many of today's popular entertainers may be nice and their songs may not be overly bad, but what are the artists saying with their lifestyles? Some of the musicians we view as wholesome make moves that are so sexually directed, we as Christians cannot possibly confuse those actions with anything other than bad taste. Not all of the songs of today's artists are bad, but because so much of it is, it is easier to listen just to good Christian music.

When I became a Christian, I had no idea that there was such a thing as contemporary Christian music. I grew up in the high energy generation, smoking weed, snorting coke, listening to funk, disco, jazz, metal, rock and R&B. When I got saved, I was not ready for "Bringing in the Sheaves." I couldn't hack Christian music, or what I thought was Christian music, so I continued listening to the radio. I identified with high energy music; it just happened to be what I liked. I couldn't wake up the day after I got saved and say that I liked the existing church music because I didn't. I heard about one or two Christian artists, but there seemed to be so little for me to identify with that I just didn't listen to a lot of Christian music.

At the same time, while attending ORU as a new Christian, I was really shocked at what Christians were listening to. I was new in this lifestyle and I had come from a completely different direction, but it was weird to walk out of my dorm room and hear a Christian listening to a song about "my big ten inch." If the Bible says you must guard your mind, letting that message in is certainly not guarding your mind.

**We have to be wise and monitor
what we listen to, to ensure that it
is the right message.**

Later while at ORU I went to a few concerts and discovered that there indeed was music in a style that I liked with the message I wanted to hear. It was still some time before I completely let go of the radio, but I eventually realized that it was difficult to listen only to uplifting music on the radio because for every two "wholesome" songs, the next one would have a message like, "If loving you is wrong, I don't want to be right" (speaking of loving a married man or woman). Now I listen to Christian music almost exclusively because there is enough of every conceivable style to satisfy just about everyone.

I try my best to ensure that the music I listen to is good seed for my mind and spirit. I watch the lifestyles of and read up on Christian and other artists because I want to know. I really don't want to listen to or support musicians, Christian or not, who don't seem to care about how they live. So many of today's Christian artists are screwed up. So many are in it for the money or use it as a stepping stone to another career in the "real" music world. I do not have a problem with a Christian who sings wholesome music in the general marketplace, but if that person becomes like the other musicians there in terms of character or morals, or if that person seeks to hide who he or she is in order to make a few bucks and to get a good record deal, I have to cancel my support. The more famous a Christian person gets, the more influence that person has to wisely advance the *cause*, so if he or she chooses to forget God, then I can only pray for that person, for I can't identify with or support him or her.

The Christian Music Market

One point I think worth making here is that I believe the Christian music industry's approach to capturing a larger market share is wrong. It is good to have Christian music played in the general marketplace because more people are there. But rather than asking the devil to give us a little more of his time to play our music, Christians should have bought radio stations and expanded their market. The more stations you own and sell on your own commercial times, the easier it is to have your music heard. Christians who have attained wealth and status in the music industry should own stations, studios and networks that allow other Christian musicians greater access to a wider listening audience.

Worship before Celebration

One thing to keep in mind when determining what to and what not to listen to is that different types of music fit different occasions. The type of music we have been discussing is largely for enjoyment and entertainment. But there is another, more important type of music we need to remember. In the Bible, worship preceded celebration. So fun music or celebration music is not the totality of music in the Kingdom.

We need to learn to praise as much as we learn to jam. We need to learn to worship before we celebrate. Our music should help us communicate with God and further our relationships with Him.

Worship is spending time in meditation with God, communicating with Him on a spiritual level that goes beyond the surface. Worship means focusing on God and His goodness and recognizing, respecting and adoring Him. We must recognize who God is and the fact that He is divine and supreme; we need to appreciate that we are His creation and that He is responsible for our very lives and existence.

Whatever the type or style of music, it should uplift, encourage, motivate and challenge us to become more like Him who is the Master, the one true Blaster. In the Book of Exodus, Miriam and the other ladies got together and celebrated with music and dancing after the Egyptians were destroyed. David also celebrated the works of the Lord.

Celebration is meant to throw off the normal mood and to become festive or happy about an event or experience. Celebration in today's world would be called having a good time. Before we party or celebrate, we should worship. With God, worship is always a priority over celebration. The music David played, on one hand, caused Saul's spirit to be lifted. On other occasions David acted "crazy" in celebration. We need to be the same way. Our music should take us higher. We need to make sure that the music we are into lifts us up.

Television and Movies

You young people like music, but you also like the visual media. People used to tell me that movies don't affect life or that television does not influence young people. Anyone with one eye and half a brain can see, without any scientific research, that things appearing on TV today are in school and on the street tomorrow. I remember as a young man on the street going to movies to see some people's blood. I used to love watching people get killed. Then when the movie was over, we got new nicknames. Sometimes a movie would appear in our town and, within a week, the same hairstyles, language and activities of the movie were in full gear on the street. Every time there is a movie about things like gangs, the Mafia, gangsters or today's lifestyles, the heroes and villains of those movies come to life even before you leave the theater.

Television and movies probably do more to form the character of young people today than any church or Christian organization.

Christians are sometimes rather slow and dumb when it comes to using the tools of the day. When radio came along, many Christians called it evil. So the devil took it over and when they wanted time on the radio, they had to buy it from people who were not interested in their message. Christians had not learned that lesson by the time television came along, because we still call TV evil today. Television is not evil; it is what's on the TV and who is controlling it that's evil. We Christians should own more stations. Then we can say more about what should be on TV. Every tool in this world can be used for good or for bad, depending upon who gets their hands on it.

Both TV and movies, however, hardly ever give an accurate or decent portrayal of Christians.

Whenever you see a program on TV about a Christian, he or she is usually portrayed as either a total square, a liar or someone who is mentally ill. The millions of us out there who are Christians must watch as our values are assaulted by a few people who probably are divorced three times, smoke grass or coke and generally have the morals of a decaying society. We know that what these people portray is not the truth. However, they do not necessarily tell the story people want to see, but rather the story the enemy wants to tell.

I like good news, but TV hardly ever shows good news. If you check out the soap operas or the dramas on TV, they seem like an endless list of people being murdered, families breaking up and relationships not working out. We get to see that every day on the daily news and in life, so why pound it in with program after program? I want to see programs about people whose lives are together, not whose lives are falling apart. Maybe the names of some of the soap operas on TV should be changed to "The Dumb and the Stupid," "As the World Regurgitates," "The Sick and the Sorry," "The Adventures of the Adulterers" or "Bad Days in Our Lives." I want to see shows with marriages that work, with young people who decide to wait until marriage to have sex and with the many happy endings I see among the young people with whom I deal. Of course, that won't happen unless moral people have an equal opportunity and own and produce materials that build up rather than tear down.

Today's Movies

At one time a PG movie meant pretty good. Now PG often means pretty gory or piece of gunk. I love movies, but

I have a real problem when I want to watch one. You see, I made a personal decision some time ago not to watch movies that have violence as a theme and that have no redeeming value. Movies rated "R" often are filled with so much garbage that if there was a message in them, you could hardly find it. The problem is, not many Christian movies are around and hardly any Christian television exists except for preaching. Today's teens, with their short attention spans, will not spend a lot of time watching preaching.

Until there is more to offer in the way of Christian film, you Christian young people who choose to watch today's movies need to be careful to choose ones that have a redeeming message or some good point to them.

The movies and television programs you watch need to be compared to the values of the Bible. If the values espoused by a movie or television program are contrary to God's Word, you as a citizen of a higher kingdom should not watch or support it. Some good movies that have positive messages are out there, but good movies are sometimes few and far between. As a Christian, you must monitor what you watch in order to guard your mind. Monitoring what you watch is certainly a difficult job, given today's choices. If I were to give advice on this subject, I would say the following:

Never watch horror or ghost movies. These movies have a direct link to satanic activity. I avoid horror, demon or ghost movies the same way I would avoid movies featuring child molesters. Satan is the god of horror and fear. Just think of how many people have recurring nightmares or fear to sleep alone as a result of these types of movies. Guard your mind and leave this stuff alone.

Movies containing strong sexual content should be avoided because God doesn't appreciate people presenting His invention in the wrong light. (Remember He invented sex and wrote the book on how it was supposed to operate.) You may have enough problems controlling your hormones as it is without being continually stimulated by sex on the big screen.

You should not watch movies that have excessive violence or that have violence as the theme. There is just no redeeming value in these movies. If you want to go places in life, they are excess baggage. The more violence you see, the easier it is to resort to violence and the less sensitive you become to the tragic effects of a violent society.

Dance and Parties

What's wrong with dancing? What's wrong with partying? Are they things God dislikes or are they things created by the devil? If God didn't like dance or if the devil created parties, then God did not authorize the celebration of the children of Israel when they crossed the Red Sea. I would imagine that there was a real party after they made it to the other side. Dance is also a part of celebration in the Bible. David danced in celebration. So did Miriam and the other women after they crossed the Red Sea. We too can dance when we have the right motive and method.

Dance can be fun, creative and as unto the Lord. But like so many other things, it gets lost in a maze of abuse of its original purpose.

Much of the dancing and partying of today has been built on the wrong foundation. Teenagers are told that, in order to have a good time, they need to be high, drunk, sexually active or rebellious. The truth is, parties are so much better when there is no alcohol, when there is no sex and when people are in their right minds. If you are not drunk, you don't throw up, you don't have a hangover and people don't get killed because of drunk driving.

I used to frequent night clubs and parties and there was a lot of celebration and dancing. After I got saved, people would ask me why I didn't go dancing and to nightclubs and parties like I had before. The fact is, I could never say that I didn't enjoy dancing or that I did not have fun. I could not even say there was something inherently wrong with moving your body. The problem is the spirit of those parties and nightclubs.

For one thing, the wrong message is being preached at those places. Yes, the world does a much better job of preaching and evangelizing than Christians; they sell their products aggressively: "shake your booty," "I want to sex you up," "saving all my love for you," "when I get that feeling I need sexual healing." The message in the music sets the stage for something that has nothing to do with God. Then there is the smoke, alcohol and drugs to alter the mood and a little wine to make the eyes red and help the ladies forget what Mamma said about what guys would do.

Many times the boys and I would go to a party or a nightclub and decide before we got there that we wanted to score. We wanted to do some slow dancing and some talking and begging so that at the end of the night our investment would pay off. Those movements on the dance floor point to one thing: sex. It was only later that I found out you can have fun without pointing to sex. You can have a party without music which points away from God and toward sex. You don't need alcohol to have a party or to have a good time.

The same law that governs the rest of our lives applies to parties or fun events: Do everything as unto the Lord. Because of what dance means in the lifes of so many, it may be better to find alternative fun activities such as: bowling, skating and fun contests. Christians can have parties that are good clean fun with Christian music, fun games and crazy activities kids enjoy, but without the excess baggage of alcohol, sex and violence.

Creative Dance

Dance is obviously a natural part of human expression just like music is. Dance can be edifying, entertaining and uplifting. If can also be nasty, ugly and a prelude to sex. Dance should not be vulgar. Satan has distorted dance just like everything else he has touched. Whatever we do, we need to find God's original purpose for it and use it for what He intended. Surely God, who invented dance, wants us to use it today to honor Him.

Dance is another tool. Teenagers will dance to some tune, whether it is the devil's music or God's music. Make sure you use something like dance for your benefit and spiritual growth.

I have seen very creative dance and drama used to draw people to the Lord. Teen Mania missions and other groups that travel around the world with teens share the good news by using contemporary music and creative dance and drama. Some of the people they reach would not listen if you approached them directly with the gospel. Dance and music are tools that get their attention so you can talk to them about the gospel.

Culture

One of today's problems is that culture and art have been confused with vulgarity. Dance does not have to look base or despicable. Sex is very private and not meant for public consumption or enticement. Whenever dance or culture incites sexual passion, it is functioning outside of its intention and is not being used as it was designed. In fact, dance or culture is then being used to advance the kingdom of satan.

One of the things we should always keep in mind about entertainment is that there is a season for everything.

Worship always comes before celebration. We should never substitute entertainment for substance. A fasted spiritual life is the first priority. Worship, as a staple in the life of the believer, should be in place before we celebrate.

Entertainment obviously is a need of all human beings, and Christians are no different. We need to party, laugh and have a good time. We cannot, however, really celebrate properly if we don't know how to worship. When we don't, our lives are unbalanced.

Points to Remember

---

1. Teens want to have fun.

2. God likes what you like.

3. God does not have a type of music that He has placed upon His Body and said, "Play this only." Christian music is more what you say than how you play.

4. God is too big to fit into a single culture, style or fashion.

5. Ensure that the music you listen to is good seed for your mind and spirit.

6. Watch the lifestyles of and read up on Christian and other artists. Don't listen to or support musicians, Christian or not, who don't seem to care about how they live.

7. We need to learn to praise as much as we learn to jam. We need to learn to worship before we celebrate.

8. Our music needs to help us communicate with God and should further our relationships with Him.

9. Television is not evil; it is what's on the TV and who is controlling it that's evil.

10. Christians should own more stations; then we can say more about what should be on television.

11. The movies and television programs you watch need to be compared to the values of

the Bible. If the values espoused by a movie or television program are contrary to God's Word, you as a citizen of a higher kingdom should not watch or support it.

12. Dance can be fun, creative and as unto the Lord. But like so many other things, it gets lost in a maze of abuse of its original purpose.

13. We should never substitute entertainment for substance.

5 Peer Pressure and Self Image

A broken young man said
"Power to the People"
A lost young man said,
"Let's live it up"
A searching lady said
"Let's get it together"
A young man who followed others said
"What up?"
They built a pyramid
of waste into the sky
each tried to impress the other
none failed and none succeeded
They experienced comfort
As they mocked each other
They tried desperately to cover up
What each of them knew...
but one young man could see through it all
He was the Wise one...

(Davy B)

Cool and the Gang

In discussing some of the characteristics of youth in Chapter One, I mentioned that youth were collaborators. Young people in search of an identity don't want to be alone or odd. Everybody wants to be cool. Kids don't want to be left out or seen as a "nerd." Teens like to impress each other. Whatever is seen as "happening," teens want to be a part of it. Nobody wants to be left out. That is normal. The problem is that what is "in" or cool in the teen world often is destructive, wrong, and in some cases, criminal.

It may be cool to listen to heavy metal, but the values portrayed in those songs are often deadly. Heavy metal musicians frequently are associated symbolically or in reality with devil worship or the promotion of sex, drugs and alcohol. Gangs also influence young people to get into drugs, violence and crime. So much of peer pressure is negative peer pressure and damages many of our young people.

Peer pressure can be positive or negative. It just so happens that in today's world peer pressure is mostly negative. Peer pressure will always exist, so you as a Christian young person need to ensure that peer pressure is used to direct friends in the right direction. Christian teens need to be strong, ruthless youth; ruthless with a cause. Many young people today are violent and vicious to the extreme. Christian youth need to be just as ruthless toward what satan perpetrates. We need to be ruthless in destroying the works of the enemy. Jesus noted that the purpose of His coming into the world was to destroy the works of the enemy. I probably would have been saved much earlier in life if stronger young people had been in the church. Teens are waiting for some youth with authority to tell and show them what life is all about; to show them that there is a better way. Your friends would want a relationship with Jesus Christ if they had an opportunity to know the truth about Him.

The Man in the Mirror

When you look at yourself, what do you see? Do you like what you see? What do you think God sees? How you see yourself, your self image, is the single most important factor in determining where you will go in life. If you see yourself as weak and as a nobody, your course has been set. (Proverbs 23:7 notes, "as a man thinketh so is he.") The less you think of yourself, the more you need the approval of others to feel worthwhile. But for you as a Christian young person, the most important thing is not how others see you, but how God sees you. If He approves of you, then you are approved. You need nothing more. These verses of Romans 8:1-2 tell us that...

Therefore, there is now no condemnation for those who are in Christ Jesus, because through Christ Jesus the law of the Spirit of life set me free from the law of sin and death.

Romans 8:37 notes that...

No, in all these things we are more than conquerors through him who loved us.

Unfortunately, teenagers are good at putting each other down. If they think you are ugly, they let you know. If they think you are cool, they let you know. If you don't know how God sees you and how important you are to Him, you will look to friends for approval. How do you see yourself? What does the man in your mirror have to say? God said we were created in His image and likeness and God is certainly not a loser.

It is amazing how the world makes Christian young people ashamed of who they are. We have the best news in the world, the best lifestyle and the best that God has to offer, yet we still feel ashamed. A guy is proud to cuss in public, but we are afraid to say "Praise the Lord." Cussing is praising the devil, so we can certainly say "Praise the Lord" if we want to. Rather than worrying about what others think, always ask yourself, "What does God think?" He thinks (knows) that He created the world, has all power and authority and does not need anyone's approval to do anything. We are His children; shouldn't we think like He thinks?

You are special. You have talents and abilities unique to you. You should never let another's opinion of you become your opinion of yourself. God made you and He doesn't make junk. Your talents, abilities or looks have nothing to do with who you really are. Some of us have talent; others don't. Regardless of what you were or were not naturally blessed with, you are cool. It is said that every human being who is born has beat the odds of one million to one. Scientists say that over a million sperm are present in the reproductory process. So out of over one million, you happened to be the one to make it. You must be special. You were born cool; you don't need someone to grade you to determine if you are cool.

Jesus is the image of God in flesh. God created us to be like Him, to have His authority and His dominion and to demonstrate His qualities. Of course, our ability to keep that image was damaged. But now we have the opportunity in Christ to regain a measure of that image (not the complete image, because the devil is in between while we are on earth). What are you supposed to see, according to God? You are supposed to see someone who looks, acts and thinks like Him! You must know who you are in Christ, or you will live for the opinion and approval of others. Walk around from day to day in school or on the job as if your Daddy owns the joint, because He does. I don't mean that you should be arrogant, but you should at least act like you belong and not act afraid or ashamed of who you are. See yourself as a winner, because God does.

It's amazing, but Jesus never seemed to be bothered by what other people thought. He knew who He was, He knew what He came to do and He didn't wait on what people thought about Him to determine what He would do. He was just cool. One time He wanted to go to Zac's house for dinner, so He just said, "Zac, I'm coming to your house for dinner, you with dat'." Zac said, "Sure, dude, whatever you say." Jesus never lost His cool and never let others' opinions of Him affect how He lived. If you are following Jesus, you should do the same. Think of yourself the way God thinks of you.

Everybody's Not Doing It

You go to school every day and people beg you to come to this party, drink this beer, be a man or woman. It's true that the pressure to give in is great, and most people will give in because they don't want to be left out. But one thing you must remember is this: If everybody's doing it, then why do they need you to do it too? The truth is, everybody is not doing it. That just happens to be the line they use to try and get you to do it. I heard a story of a girl who was approached by a young sweet talker for sex and he brought her the same line: "Everybody's doing it." She told him, "Well, if everybody is doing it, then you certainly have a lot of other choices because I am certainly not doing it."

Even if everybody is doing it, that doesn't mean it's right. It's difficult to stand up to pressure, but think of what a challenge it is and the wonderful results you achieve in the end. The Bible tells the story of three youths who were told by Nebucadnezzer that everybody's doing it. They stood up and said, "Yo Neb, we're not doing it. Our God is able to deliver us and even if He doesn't, we won't play your game."

It may be easy to give in now, but it is hard when you have to live for nine months asking yourself why. It may be easy to smoke that joint or hit some cocaine, but it is not easy when you are hooked and there seems to be no way out. Saying "no" now is a lot easier than saying "no" later. Rehabilitation from alcohol takes a lifetime; saying "no" now takes two seconds. Remember, truth is not determined by numbers. Truth speaks for itself. It takes courage to be different, but the rewards are much greater.

Positive Peer Pressure

If you have set standards and goals for your life, don't be distracted by what others think and say. Fight the pressure. Fight the illegitimate power. In fact, not only should you fight the pressure, you should also reverse the pressure where appropriate. There is power in numbers, so get the numbers on your side. Hang out with people who have the same vision and mission that you have. If others invite you to their party, say "No, I can't make it. Why don't you come to mine?" Invite your friends over to your house and talk to them one-on-one. Let them know where you stand and let them know there is a better way for them.

Sometimes we are afraid of being too evangelistic. The truth is, evangelism is not something that only Christians do. Gangs go out and evangelize a school; drug dealers go out and evangelize the block. They preach their message and invite, sometimes even by force, others to come and join them. If they are not ashamed to do it, why should we? We should be less ashamed because we know we are right. Of course, you don't want to obnoxious about it. Make friends and then invite them to take a look at what you have found.

It's not up to you to convince your friends that what you have is real; that's God's part. Just share what you know. Invite them to your youth meeting or church. They will invite you to their parties or whatever else they are into. Share with them the simple biblical plan of salvation. Tell them that those who have not accepted what Jesus has provided are separated from God. By simply confessing our sins, repenting and accepting Jesus as Lord and Savior, we regain our spiritual relationship to God through the new birth. The first birth means we come into the world separated from God because of sin and man's fallen nature. The second birth means we are reunited with God and sin no longer separates us from Him. But whenever possible, keep the numbers on your side by having your friends with you in a group situation when you talk to others about the Lord.

Power or Purpose

Above everything else, you need to know where you are going in life. You need to know why you believe and live the way you do. If you know your purpose, then it is difficult for abuse to occur. Abuse occurs when you don't know the purpose of something. As a Christian, you should know the purpose of life, why God made you and where He wants you to go. When you know what you want out of life, when you know where you are going and have made plans, it is a lot more difficult for the things around you and for the games people play to distract you. The people who encourage you to do the wrong things often have no direction in life. If you ask them what their plans for life are, they will probably say, "I don't know, man, I just want to relax for awhile." Some never stop "relaxing." These people don't pay your bills. When you have real problems, they won't be around.

You are, first and foremost, an individual. Look out for your best interests. Determine what you need to do and what God desires for your life, then pursue it with all your might. It is in your best interest to do what the One who made you said to do. Anything less than His best is less than you could be.

When you know who you are and where you are going, you can live above what people think, be it criticism or praise. It is good to know what people think, but if you live for their approval, you rob yourself of your potential for greatness. Many times young people and adults confuse popularity with being loved. The world often is a very cold place. The things you do can cause you to believe everyone loves you, but you soon discover that if you don't continue to succeed, you are quickly forgotten. Athletes and entertainers often make this mistake. A good basketball player plays well all year and everybody loves him, or so he thinks. Then he has a few bad games and in the biggest game of his career, he plays terribly and is booed off the court. The same people who "loved" him yesterday "hate" him today.

Never be moved by people's criticism; otherwise you will hate yourself and never feel good enough. Never be moved by their praise, either. When they praise you, you feel really good. But what do you do when there is no applause and no one around? Be driven by your purpose and by the plans you have made. *Establish some goals for your life: spiritually, physically and mentally.* Learn to be gracious in both the high times and the low times. However, don't disregard people's opinions altogether; being observed can help you to grow. But if you live for what people say, you will grow or shrink depending upon who is talking to you.

Destined to Win

God does not create losers. He doesn't make junk and He does not plan a future for you which intends you to be a loser. When you are born again, you are born again to win. A popular song of years ago stated that we are "destined to win." That is so true. *God does not destine failures. He sets us up to win.* You can decide to become a loser by accepting things that are less than God's best, but you don't have to. If being cool means using drugs or getting into trouble, you can do without being cool. Believing that you are not destined to win leads you into a path where you follow the wrong people.

If you believe in God at all, you must know that He would not want you to come into the world without purpose and end up as a miserable failure. He has planned success for you. God's success may not always be the easy way out though. Living right sometimes causes you to lose things or friends you may hold dear. In the end, however, His way is the best. I know because I have been there.

As a teen, I couldn't wait to be cool and be tough. I saw the drug dealers, the guys with so many ladies, and I couldn't wait. So I got a quick start. I started getting high at the age of twelve. I got in fights and quickly moved into the big time at school. I went to school with weed and pills to sell and distribute. "Davy B" had arrived. Other students took their geometry sets to school full of geometry instruments. Mine was full of drugs of one kind or the other. I didn't get in fights with just students either. I cussed out and physically attacked teachers.

After school I hung out on the street. I roamed Harlem and Warren Street (Nassau) day and night as a young boy. I thought that was fun; I thought I had arrived. I learned to make the moves on the ladies. I just followed the older guys. Time and time again I exercised the art of sweet talking ladies for sex. I fell right into the program. It was always, "Let's do this. Let's do that." You name it, I did it.

It's funny how you think you are right and everything is cool...then reality comes knocking at your door and says "Hello." Mr. Reality showed up on me while I was having a good time. The police car signalled to my friend and me to pull over. Of course we couldn't. We had an ounce of weed in the car and were cruising through town smoking away. They insisted. Soon lights were flashing, rubber was burning and the chase was on. Eventually we got caught, handcuffed and escorted to a wonderful jail cell. The cell didn't have any bed. Four of us were in one cell. Fingerprints were taken, there were questions. I did not go to jail, but I did spend that night thinking about what my mother used to say about God. How did I come to this?

I did not learn the answer right away. I ended up in the same position again before I realized that I was living for someone else's approval. Once again I found myself in the presence of the law, contemplating how much time I might have to spend in jail. Fortunately, the time came when I realized I had to make some decisions for myself. I had to make some decisions for Davy B. Through the help of a Christian friend who explained to me what God had planned for my life if I would accept His plan, I decided that God was right and accepted the Lord.

I went back to those same friends and they still said, "Come on, man, try this or do that." But things had changed; I knew who I was. I was no longer the influenced. I would not let them sway me. I hung around the same guys for a time, then realized we were going in different directions. So I left. I kept living my life and they kept living theirs, but they watched me and one by one, when they reached low points in their own lives, they admitted, "Davy B, what you've got is real." Not many of them got saved, but they knew I was a winner and understood the reason for it. So you don't have to defend God. Your friends need to defend their sin. God never loses and never fails.

Points to Remember

1. Teenagers want to be cool. Kids don't want to be left out or seen as a "nerd."

2. How you see yourself is the single most important factor in determining where you will go in life.

3. Young people who don't know how God sees them and how important they are to Him look to friends for approval.

4. The truth is, everybody is not doing it. That just happens to be the line they use to get you to do it.

5. Peer pressure can be positive or negative. In today's world, peer pressure happens to be mostly negative.

6. Not only should you fight the pressure, you should also reverse the pressure where appropriate.

7. God does not destine failures. He sets us up to win.

8. When you know what you want out of life and know where you are going and have made plans, it is a lot more difficult for the things around you and for the games people play to distract you.

9. Evangelism is not something that only Christians do. Gangs go out and evangelize

a school; drug dealers go out and evangelize the block. They preach their message and invite, sometimes even by force, others to come and join them.

10. It may be easy to give in now, but it is hard when you must live for nine months asking yourself why. It may be easy to smoke that joint or hit some cocaine, but it is not easy when you are hooked and there seems to be no way out. Saying "no" now is a lot easier than saying "no" later.

11. Look into God's Word and discover your reason and purpose for living. Once you know His purpose for your life, your course will be clear.

6 Drug Abuse and Self Control

Your Drug of Choice comes in a bottle
Mine comes in a pipe
We sit here arguing
Which one is wrong or right
Johnny died yesterday
OD'ed on coke
Susie's last ride was an accident
The driver drank as a joke
How many of us will die
How many mothers will cry
How many human beings will fry
because of dope...

(Davy B)

Wine is a mocker and beer a brawler; whoever is led astray by them is not wise (Proverbs 20:1).

Do not join those who drink too much wine or gorge themselves on meat, for drunkards and gluttons become poor, and drowsiness clothes them in rags (Proverbs 23:20-21).

Who has woe? Who has sorrow? Who has strife? Who has complaints? Who has needless bruises? Who has bloodshot eyes? Those who linger over wine, who go to sample bowls of mixed wine. Do not gaze at wine when it is red, when it sparkles in the cup, when it goes down smoothly! In the end it bites like a snake and poisons like a viper. Your eyes will see strange sights and your mind imagine confusing things. You will be like one sleeping on the high seas, lying on top of the rigging. "They hit me," you will say, "but I'm not hurt! They beat me, but I don't feel it! When will I wake up so I can find another drink?" (Proverbs 23:29-35).

It sounds like Solomon is still living today. God recognized the dangers of drugs before we knew there was such a thing and had Solomon write these words for our benefit. This passage is so graphic and to the point. Does it not describe what we see every day of our lives? Yet we are too smart to listen to wisdom. We have deceived ourselves into believing we know better, that we can handle it. "No problem."

Drugs need no introduction today. We have all been affected by them either directly or indirectly. Most of us probably have been affected directly. It is said that 85 percent of high school students experimented with some type of drug before they reached the age of 15. Why? What is it about this life that causes young people to seek to get high? Why can't they see the danger and decide to say no? Dealing with drugs or, as they say, substance abuse, is also very interesting.

Alcohol and other drugs probably are involved in every problem that happens in our society, whether it is adultery, rape, armed robbery or murder. There is something about drugs that alters a person's state of normalcy and encourages him or her to be abnormal, abusive or even criminal.

How many times have we seen situations like this one: A young girl goes to a party. The married man she saw out of the corner of her eye was a little "juiced." He noticed her stare and was turned on. The young lady had also had some drinks, so she was a little juiced. They talked. He seemed so handsome to her. The night went on. When he went home and beat his wife, he was still a little juiced. Nine months later the young girl had the baby and she thought, "If I hadn't had any drinks that night, I wouldn't have succumbed." Her son grows up without a father, gets high with the boys, gets his girlfriend pregnant and then leaves.

As this story shows, drugs have a hand in every problem in one way or another. Man's heart is sinful and he will find a way to sin regardless of which drug is available. But the availability and promotion of drugs in our societies accelerates the destruction of teenagers. The cycle goes on and on.

Drugs are big business. Estimates on the annual intake from drugs and alcohol combined account for more money than any other industry in the world. People of all ages, social backgrounds and persuasions in life become ensnared by drugs. Drugs are a vital part of almost every society in the world. The worst part is that our youth and their vast potential are being sapped daily by this monster. Yet we do nothing, or very little, to really stop drug use. So young men attending a party are encouraged by peers to drink in order to build up their courage to dance. Alcohol is advertised every day: "This Bud's for You," "The World Is a Very Cool Place," "The Right Beer Now."

You are being sold a story every day about drugs and alcohol. Of course, only the "good" side is presented.

"Try this, this is some mean stuff...if you don't you are a faggot...." That is the world you must grow up in. It is weird, but drug abuse seems to be a part of man, even a need.

After the ballgame or even during the ballgame, we must have a beer. We toast to our health with alcohol, we celebrate with alcohol. Sexy ladies advertise the benefits of alcohol for us. We drive with alcohol and we die with alcohol and other drugs. Most fatal accidents involve alcohol or some other drug. And the beat goes on and on.

The funny thing is, despite all the death, the best we do is tell kids to "Just Say No" when everything else we do and say points to "Just Say Yes" or you're not cool. People want to prosecute teens and others for drunk driving, yet they don't want to tell teens not to drink. I mean, if alcohol does so much harm to so many people, it would stand to reason that we ought to discourage people from using it. There is no reason we should see the heavy promotion of such a dangerous drug. At the very least, companies that sell alcohol should heavily promote the use of nonalcoholic beer.

If you are not telling people not to drink, then don't tell them not to smoke grass or use cocaine. Your chosen drug may happen to come in a can that is called beer; another person's chosen drug may come in a tube or a cellophane bag. One of the stupidest things I have ever seen in my life is a wine event to raise money to fight drugs. How about selling joints to raise money to fight alcohol or selling cigarettes to fight lung cancer?

Why Do Teens Get High?

Teens don't understand their purpose.

Today too many young people both in the church and outside have no reason for living. They live from day to day without a plan for their lives. They don't understand exactly who they are or why they are here, so they drift. Someone comes along and says, "Let's do this" or "Try this, man, you'll be cool." Just the mere fact of having some kind of plan for your life and knowing who you are will tell you that drugs are to be avoided. If early in your life you set clear goals and plan on a given career, you must recognize that drugs are guaranteed to derail the very best of plans. If you set spiritual goals for your life, the use of drugs is automatically eliminated. God will never plan for you to destroy your life.

Teens are lovers of pleasure.

Teens love to have fun and want to be seen as being cool. Drugs and alcohol are advertised as being fun, but the side effects are clearly disguised and are purposely not advertised. Indeed, drugs and alcohol do have an aspect of pleasure, or they wouldn't be so attractive. One of the sad realities of our society is that we not only like to have fun, we also don't seem to care if it kills us. It seems that society encourages and condones fun without responsibility, as if we can go on forever doing whatever we like and nothing will happen. The message is that fun is drinking beer, using drugs and having free sex. Eat, drink and be merry, for tomorrow we die. (Haven't we heard that before?)

Over and over we see the same results, and yet another generation grows up and repeats the process. Teens will always love to have fun, and there is nothing wrong with having fun. The problem is when we confuse fun with destructiveness and irresponsibility. We all love to have fun and have a good time. It is not necessary to kill yourself in the process.

Teens have never learned responsibility.

Many young people who get hooked on drugs are those who learned irresponsibility. They shirked responsibilities at home, then at school, then at work and eventually they only want to party and play. They refuse to study, refuse to work, refuse to obey, refuse to pray. How many people do you know who live for the weekend? "Thank God it's Friday;

where's the party, dude?" Without the will and the courage to live life the way it was planned, they become easy prey to an experience they will never forget.

Years later these same persons are left without a future because they never learned the value of responsibility. If you check the rehabilitation centers around the world, they all have one thing in common: people who never grew up, who never learned to be responsible during their early years. There is a time for everything under the sun, so there surely is a time for us to be responsible.

Teens believe the hype.

Satan has obviously been successful in distorting the truth. He has produced a garbage list that so many of our young people have bought. Youth are made to believe that they need certain things in order to be men and women. They say you haven't really grown up until you have a bottle of beer in your hand or some fine liquor for the lady of "distinction" (more like "extinction"). The movie and television screens show you that real men can drink and handle it without a problem. You are told that in order to be cool, you must be part of the "new breed" who smoke only the best "weed." And if you are really tough, you can handle cocaine. Only soft guys get hooked, they say. So the lifestyles of drug dealers are glamorized every day. The hype is on.

Teens are followers.

If everybody's doing it, then why are you not doing it? Most teens value the safety of the group and bow to the pressure so they can be included, even if it means using drugs or engaging in unsound activities. It is difficult to go against the crowd. It is difficult to be unpopular. Most teens are followers, wanting to please others. How do you feel when you are called "soft," "wimp" or "sissy"? The natural reaction is to prove the others wrong, that you are tough. These are some of the reasons young women and men use drugs. Most people follow trends. That is so evident among youth with new styles, new fashions, new haircuts and, of course, new drugs.

How the Battle Is Won: Preventing Youth Drug Abuse

Establish self control early.

Discipline is the one thing most young people hate and love at the same time. But the later in life you learn discipline, the harder it is to overcome bad habits. In my work with drug addicts, I have noticed one thing that most of those who are unable to conquer their habit have in common: They never learned simple discipline. They spent years giving in to the pressure, not being able to say no to anything destructive. When they enter rehabilitation, they are actually encountering real discipline for the first time in 15 or 20 years.

Discipline is inevitable. Groups like Teen Challenge have no magic solution; they simply teach discipline, responsibility and purpose as shown in the Book. They simply show addicts what they should have been doing all along. It should be evident to you by now that one of the greatest sources of simple wisdom for daily living is the Book of Proverbs. Check out this verse of Proverbs:

Like a city whose walls are broken down is a man who lacks self-control (25:28).

It is difficult to turn around a lifestyle which lacks discipline in three months or even in three years. The longer you wait to establish self control when you need to, the harder it is. If you don't stand for something, you fall for anything. Decide what is right and wrong. Decide what will benefit you and what will bring you down and follow the path of self control. Self control means looking at what "The Maker" says about the way your life should run and planning to live by it. Self control comes from a personal, active relationship with Jesus Christ.

Only God can help you live the way you should. Only He who wrote the book on life can sustain you in life and in the trials you face. Without prayer, Bible study and fellowship with people of like mind, self control becomes harder and harder. If you choose the right way, you will be the one who has the advantage as life goes on. People who escape discipline and self control often slowly but surely kill themselves. Sometimes not slowly at all.

Take responsibility.

In this world in which we live, it seems young men are taught to be responsible less than young ladies are because of so many absent fathers. Many young men lack that authority or covering they need to learn responsibility. So they begin living a pattern of irresponsibility. They go out and play while their sister and mother keep the house in order. They learn how to have sex but not how to be a parent. As soon as they find out the girl is pregnant, they vanish, running away from responsibility. Young men learn so much about playing games and hanging out that when it comes to facing the serious challenges of life, they are unable to handle it.

Young men must be young men and not jive-time fools. Any animal can have sex. Dogs, cats, tigers, monkeys—any animal. Sex is no big deal. Men are not supposed to be dogs. We don't just get "in heat" and head for the border to satisfy an appetite. There are responsibilities that go along with our physical appetites. If you ate every time you were hungry, some of you would weigh 600 pounds. You learn to manage your appetites. Drug and sex appetites can also be controlled by your choice to be responsible.

Young men need to learn that they should prepare now for the time when they will be called upon to lead a family.

Young men need to know their roles in family and in society. The more responsible you are now, the more you will achieve later in life and the less problems you will end up in. Young ladies, you need to know that responsibility means making sure you are ready to bring children into a whole family before you have them. Too many young ladies today are doing the very same things that have destroyed the young men. They have sex without commitment and children without a family and run from relationship to relationship without considering the consequences.

I understand a survey was done some years ago that indicated young men who had gone through a program like the Boy Scouts, which taught discipline, responsibility and survival, were less likely than any other group to end up in prison. We need strong, mature, tough young men who will take responsibility and not run from it. Stealing from your family, getting girls pregnant and running away is not being tough. Abusing drugs and alcohol is not being tough. Any fool can destroy his life and the lives of others. Really tough men build up others and lead the way rather than run away.

Focus on the rewards of discipline.

One of the fallacies of this life and of these times is that we as a society focus on the negatives of discipline and not on the rewards. However, we do recognize and promote the value and benefit of doing the right thing.

We should not even have to say that alcohol and drugs are stupid, but the rewards of these foolish activities are promoted so well that most of our young people believe they need these things.

The truth is, if there were not another drop of alcohol or drugs on the planet, we would not miss it. I found out when I stopped drinking alcohol how good apple juice tasted. I discovered how much easier it is to breathe when I stopped smoking grass and tobacco. Life is so much more fun when you don't have to look over your shoulder and wonder who is out to get you. Life is good and rewarding just the way it is. We don't need to add one thing to it.

It is sad that Christians believe fun is something for someone else. Some believe that God sits in Heaven with a fun meter and if you go over two on a scale of ten, he zaps you. It is so much easier and so much more fun to party when you know there is no ulterior motive in the shadows, no hangovers or OD's to worry about. The truth is, the life of a drug dealer is hard. I know, I personally have been there and have lived around drug dealers. They have to work hard to protect their investments. They have to watch out for friends, the police and their girlfriends. Life can be real short for the drug dealer. Dying is hard work. God's way is much more fun and much more rewarding. Kids just need to know.

Understand addicts.

When you have a brother or a friend on drugs, it's not the person that you need to attack. Your brother, sister or friend is a victim of his or her own lack of discipline and lack of understanding of why God made him or her. God did not make us to become garbage cans that inhale smoke and drink poison. He created these wonderful bodies that we have to be healthy, strong and productive.

We need to understand that these people who fell into satan's trap need love and direction. They don't need you to be soft. Being soft is what messed them up in the first place. You have to be tough. But you must love the addict and not the addiction. By the time they have become really addicted to any type of drug, the pleasure in it has long gone. Even for them the taking of that drug is a painful experience. We must work with them, help them find help, share the Word and pray for them. We may need to insist that they go into a resident rehabilitation program where they have time to rethink their existence away from the daily pressures of life.

An addict needs love and direction, not pity. They need the truth and not sympathy. They need discipline and not excuses. When you notice sudden changes in behavior, such as new friends who seem secretive, a need for money all the time, red eyes, teeth which are changing color, nervousness and abnormal agitation, it's time to talk about help.

Reverse peer pressure.

As a society and especially as the church, we need to present a different image. We need to let friends know that some of the most successful athletes of all time are Christians: A.C. Green, Barry Saunders, Terry Cummings, Mark Price, Reggie White, Dr. J, and the list goes on. Everybody is not doing it. There are hundreds and thousands of young men and women who refuse to bow to the idols of today. They play hard and tough, but when the game is over, they do not run back to the hotel to get high or to have sex with some girl who is ready to give them AIDS. No, they go to church, they have fun with their families and they enjoy sex just as much as anyone else—with their wives.

The truth is, the toughest men don't need to drink, they don't need to abuse women, they don't need to hang out in gangs. They hang out with God's posse. They know how to live the right way. They know how to have fun the right way, they know how to party the right way, they are ready for anything that comes because they walk like the Master, the one true Blaster, Jesus Christ who was and is "tougher than nails." We must let teens know that there is a better way, a way much better than the hype of today.

Tell the truth about drugs and alcohol.

What we see on television and in the movies is not the truth about drugs and alcohol. The way drugs are portrayed, you would swear they lead to a permanent good time, without any side effects. The truth is, alcohol and drugs cut short the lives of more young men and women than any other disease. More young people are dying of drunken driving accidents than you would care to know. More young people commit suicide, get pregnant, drop out of school and die as a result of alcohol and drugs than any other single factor. We never hear the truth though. Instead we hear, "If you want be really cool, drink this cool beer." Why must they lie to you. Alcohol-producing companies and drug dealers kill more young people and adults than any war in this century, or any other century. Alcohol and drugs are a crutch for a weak and undisciplined generation of boys and girls who must be told the truth. The Bible so clearly shows the deception of these killers of human potential.

> "It is not for kings, O Lemuel—not for kings to drink wine, not for rulers to crave beer, lest they drink and forget what the law decrees, and deprive all the oppressed of their rights. Give beer to those who are perishing, wine to those who are in anguish; let them drink and

forget their poverty and remember their misery no more"
(Proverbs 31:4-7).

For the most part I have, in this discussion, separated drugs and alcohol, but in reality they are one and the same. They are the same thing, the same monster. Does it matter whether you get bitten by a bear or a lion? The result is the same in both instances. Just because one is legal does not mean it is right or any different from the other.

Present Jesus.

Most young people don't know the truth about Jesus. Jesus was and is God in the flesh. He was not soft by any means. How can God be soft? He made the world. He can do anything He wants, and yet our societies have portrayed Jesus as a skinny, soft dude with sheep around His neck.

Fishermen like Peter and John would not have followed a soft dude.

Jesus was so tough that He knew He could physically take on anyone at any time, yet the only time He lifted a finger is when He met people gambling and ripping off others in the Temple. He had to be tough in order to run the Jews out of the Temple, where they were making money. He had to be tough to carry the cross. He was never afraid of human beings, never backed down when questioned and even told Herod a thing or two when Herod and Pilate had the power to let Him go. Jesus was so full of purpose and responsibility that He did not take the easy way out. He went the distance so you and I could be free.

The truth is, there was and is no man tougher than Jesus. He would walk for miles, He would get up early and stay up all night to pray. His father Joseph was a carpenter and they had no power tools. He could not go down to Sears and buy a power saw. He worked with His hands. Jesus knew how to handle ladies too. They followed Him, He taught them, He helped them accomplish and see their purpose. He never abused or demeaned ladies. Young ladies were His friends. Mary, Martha and others knew a real man when they saw him.

Jesus is the answer. His words are true. Thousands and millions of young people all over the world know that He is the Master. If you present Jesus and His Word accurately, your friends will see because they want to know the truth. We must let other young men and women know the truth, over and over, because they get the wrong messages every day. They don't get the truth from television or from music. You must present it to them, using every avenue possible and not letting any opportunity slip away.

Points to Remember

---

1. Most young people don't understand their purpose in life.

2. Teens love to have fun and drugs are promoted as fun.

3. Youths who abuse drugs have never learned responsibility.

4. Kids who abuse drugs believe the hype about the value of drugs.

5. Teens follow very easily.

6. Decide what is right and wrong. Decide what will benefit you and what will bring you down. Then follow the path of self control.

7. The more responsible you are now, the more you will achieve later in life and the less problems you will end up in.

8. We must focus on the rewards of discipline.

9. We must have compassion for other young people who have fallen into satan's trap and give them love and direction.

10. Young people need to know that some of the most successful athletes of all times are Christians.

11. The truth must be told about the destructiveness of drugs and alcohol.

**12. We must present the true picture of Jesus
to youth, using every avenue possible and
not letting any opportunity slip away.**

7 The Young and the Violent

Babies Having Babies
Kids on Crack
Who's Gonna Show them
the way to Act
Cause when they go to school
Everyday
they have to pray
That they won't be Blown away

I know there's gat to be something Better
I know there has to be
I know there's something more
Than Reality

I'm searching for a Better Way
In Life
I know there's a Better Way
...Jesus is the Better Way

(System 3)

My son, if sinners entice you, do not give in to them. If they say, "Come along with us; let's lie in wait for someone's blood, let's waylay some harmless soul; let's swallow them alive, like the grave, and whole, like those who go down to the pit; we will get all sorts of valuable things and fill our houses with plunder; throw in your lot with us, and we will share a common purse"—my son, do not go along with them, do not set foot on their paths (Proverbs 1:10-15).

Here we go again with the wisdom of the Book. God knew about violence and youth before the world was created. Nothing under the sun is new to Him. The world you live in today is vastly more violent than any generation or time in memory or recorded history. I read about gangs years ago and thought, "My, that was horrible," but nothing matches or even comes close to the violence of today. I remember reading *The Cross and the Switchblade* some years ago and thinking, "What a way to grow up." The book detailed Nicky Cruz's experiences on the streets of New York as a gang leader and how he made the turn from being a savage gang member to becoming a member of a new gang, whose leader is Jesus Christ. He detailed some pretty sick events and I thought, "What a way to live." Then when I take a look at today's teens, I realize Nicky Cruz must look back and say, "Did I ever have it good."

Gangs are no longer child's play or fun and games. Gangs are murderous organizations run by children whose parents grew up without direction. The fact that gang violence is so senseless does not seem to deter many young men, and to a certain extent women, who grow up anticipating the day they can join and wear their "colors."

How did we come to this, you may ask?

The truth is, as a society that refused to read the Book and to listen to the Maker, or read the manufacturer's manual, we planned it this way.

You may say, "Are you kidding?" No one would plan to live like that or to have young people so screwed up. But it was planned when murder became entertainment nightly and on the big screen. It was planned when the decision was made for everybody, except Christian youth, to have a right to do anything in school. It was planned when society said, "You can drink alcohol all you want, just don't drive afterwards." It was planned when people decided that not committing adultery and fornication was old fashioned and that kids don't really need a family. The truth is, this whole scenario was planned and the next episodes are being planned right now.

They don't tell you not to have sex. They assume that all teens are dumb and will automatically jump at the opportunity to have sex, get pregnant, have an abortion and live unhappily ever after. Young people are violent, especially young men. They are fruit from seeds planted years ago. Chaos in the family brings chaos in society and chaos in society breeds violence. The big question is, how do young people and adults deal with this situation? How do we save some of our friends from this path of destruction? Who will teach and show the way to go?

Positive Strokes

Gangs massage the ego of young people. When a family is disoriented and disorganized, kids don't receive attention or love. It is a fact of teen life that teens communicate less and less with parents and look more and more to a support group of peers for love, attention and most of all, acceptance. Gangs substitute for the love and caring of parents and for the positive strokes we all desire. One of the things I noticed after I left the street, or "the blocks" as we say in Nassau, is that everybody has a nickname: "Sasquatch," "Fly," "Poker," "Shaft," "Slick." Hardly anyone is called by their full name. In fact, the only time I really knew the names of some of the guys I hung out with was when they were arrested or got in trouble.

Nicknames are positive strokes. They give you the identity and reputation that you desire and must maintain.

You don't sit at home and have your parents say to you as a teen, "Johnny, you are a the coolest of the cool; you have all the young ladies on your case." Once you are given a nickname or once you have earned one, it's difficult to break away. You don't make new friends overnight. As a teen, it felt so good for me to hang out with the boys. I couldn't wait until school was out to hang out on the blocks or in the "hood" as they would say today.

The Cool, the Space and the Wack

One of the interesting phenomenon of the street, blocks or hood is the roles you get thrust into. On the street and in the hood you must have a reputation. There are three main types of reputations, but they basically revolve around the following:

"Cool" is the guy who is slick with ladies. He gained his reputation by having a lot of girls, dressing up real nice and being the life of the party. He is always talking sweet and on the lookout for pretty girls.

"*Space*" is the guy who likes to get high. Whenever you see him, he is ready to smoke some reefer, do some crack or drop some pills. He built his reputation by the way he handles drugs.

"*Wack*" is the guy who likes to fight. Wherever he goes, he is looking for action. If you say the wrong word to him, he is ready to "throw down." He built his reputation by fighting.

Of course these roles are sometimes combined, but often there is a distinct territory within which identity and reputation are gained. Once you gain a reputation on the street, you have to live up to it or you lose it. You have to keep on fighting or you lose your rank. You have to keep taking advantage of ladies or you lose your reputation.

Church Boys

One reason I found it difficult to get saved is church boys were, and still are, considered soft. When I was young, my mother made me go to church. As I got older, I was so ashamed of having to go to church that when I passed the street where they guys used to hang out on Sunday mornings, I would lie down in the car and hide so they wouldn't see me. None of my boys went to church so I felt a little silly. After awhile I stopped going to church. Church boys just did not seem like they knew "what time it is."

I was so affected by this mentality that even when I got saved I really could not "hang" with the church boys. They were really square, they were nerds. After church, I would still go and hang out with the group that I had come to identify with over the years, the brothers. Not until I couldn't take it anymore, being around drugs and being jeered at, did I leave. I finally realized that I couldn't "hang" anymore. What is sad is that some church boys truly were not very strong. On the other hand, it is still generally a lie perpetrated by the father of lies.

Being a Christian and going to church has nothing to do with your physical toughness, strength or coolness. In fact, church young people should be stronger and bolder because they have the answers to life.

Physical violence has nothing to do with being tough.

By the way, church guys can lift weights, carry weapons and be violent if they want to. But who needs that? Where you hang out has nothing to do with whether you are tough or not. People had, and still have, a misconception about Jesus and physical toughness. The disciples were rough dudes. Peter used to carry a machete (sword) and he used it when they came to mess with his "home boy" (Jesus). These guys were fishermen and tax collectors. Fishermen and tax collectors don't follow a soft guy. Jesus had to constantly tell His disciples that His Kingdom was not of this world because they were ready to fight the Romans and take over when the time came. He had to tell them He was into a different type of violence: one on a higher level.

Nobody's Tough

There is no such thing as a tough guy. Violence kills the good, the bad, the ugly, the not-so-bad and the innocent. Violence has no logic other than to destroy God's creation.

One thing we must get straight in our heads is that only one tough Man ever walked the face of the earth. You see, you are not tough until you can pass the ultimate test. The ultimate test is whether or not you can die and come back. Only one Man passed the ultimate test: Jesus Christ.

If you can die, you are not tough yet. Over and over again I have seen guys who thought they were so tough, they intimidated a whole neighborhood. Then one day some-body came along and *decided* they weren't so tough. "My main man bit the dust." You see, no one is really tough. It's just a matter of decision. A "bad" dude can come along and mess with people and they'll do nothing. One day, however, some person will decide that he or she has had enough. That simple decision, made in the mind of a man or woman, just ended the life of the "bad dude." Guns have made us all equal. The only thing that separates one from the other is a decision. A ten-year-old boy can make a decision and, with a gun in his hand, he can command the "baddest" guy on the block to kiss the dirt.

Physical violence is not being tough. Being tough is standing up for what's right, regardless of who is with you. You stand your ground because you have no doubt as to who God is and who is in charge.

Without Cause

Violence becomes, at the end of a day, a very vicious cycle. Violence is often without real cause or purpose. "They hurt my buddy, so I'm gonna kill them." It is amazing that criminals will lie, cheat, steal and kill, but if it happens to them or to someone in their family, they go crazy, as if it was something new which they hadn't seen before. Violence to many young men is a rite of passage. You arrive when you can take care of business. This stage often brings about senseless violence.

Nobody ever wins. In fact, nobody ever really knows why he is fighting. You wear blue and I wear red, so we fight. You live on this block and I live on that block, so we fight.

When we change addresses but still live in the same area, we who were enemies become friends. Young men often feel their "hormones" and want to flex their muscles. Some guys "get off" by chasing women. Others "get off" by beating up people. If you are a teen, you don't need violence.

Violence should be the very last resort and should occur only when you must defend yourself and have used up all other options. Let the police and other authorities do their jobs. At the very least, you should report those who may harass you to the authorities before you take anything into your own hands. God does not want us seeking vengeance. He said vengeance belongs to Him. Most young people only think of the giving end of violence and not the receiving end. It is okay for you to beat up someone or injure someone and brag about it, but what happens when you yourself end up in the hospital or morgue because of senseless violence? If you give it, you can guarantee that one day you will receive it. The Book says that if you live by the sword, you will die by it.

The Truth about Violence

The truth about violence is that it has become a part of everyday life. Violence is with us. The sadder truth is that nobody benefits from violence. People die day after day and nothing is gained. We don't need to be violent. As Christians, we are taught that violence is just not a part of our lifestyles. Violence is absolutely a last resort. You can control your temper and you don't need to retaliate when angry or offended. Some people will say, "I can't help it." Yet if someone slaps you and pulls out a gun, you can help it then. Self control is a decision you make based upon God's Word and not on how you feel.

Jesus could have been violent. He chose not to be violent. If He had decided to, Jesus could have physically brutalized the many idiots who crossed His path on a daily basis.

Jesus probably had extreme physical strength because He actually ran the Pharisees out of the Temple when they were making money there. You have to be tough to run people away from their money. Jesus actually took a whip, ran them out and turned over the tables. Yet in spite of His physical strength, He ignored threats and insults because He had a higher goal in mind. If you want to be tough, you can't be concerned about the petty things with which your friends may be concerned.

We are supposed to be like Jesus. His purpose and goal were so uppermost in His mind that even the cross and death could not persuade Him to give up (Hebrews 12:1-3).

We have the same opportunity to follow the easy way out and hang with fools as we do to take the higher road and be like Jesus, who is tougher than nails.

The only one who really wins with violence is satan, as he ends the life of another person born in God's image and who had the potential to be something great. The toughest guy is the one who can be responsible in the face of adversity. Tough guys can face a challenge and win the battle. Tough guys can take the message to a confused and sick generation, carrying the most powerful weapon of all: the Book. Ignoring guns, threats and insults, these new tough guys are making their presence felt all over the world by choosing to follow the only tough Man who ever lived, the only One to die and come back: Jesus.

Points to Remember

---

1. A society that refused to read the Book and listen to the Maker, or read the manufacturer's manual, by default planned the violence that exists.

2. Young people are violent, but they are fruit from seeds planted years ago.

3. Gangs substitute for the love and caring of parents and for the positive strokes we all desire.

4. Nicknames are positive strokes. They give you the identity and reputation that you must maintain.

5. Being a Christian and going to church has nothing to do with your physical toughness, strength or coolness.

6. Only one tough Man ever walked the face of the earth. Only one Man passed the ultimate test, died and came back: Jesus.

7. Guns have made us all equal. The only thing that separates one from the other is a decision.

8. The Book says that if you live by the sword, you will die by it. Most young people think only of the giving end of violence and not of the receiving end.

9. Jesus could have been violent. He chose not to be violent. We are supposed to be like Him.

10. Jesus kept His purpose and goal in mind so much that even the cross and death could not persuade Him to give up.

11. The only one who really wins with violence is satan, as he ends the life of another person born in God's image and who had the potential to be something great.

8 Let's Get Busy

JC said Get Busy
He didn't say how
What he did say
is to it now
Don't wait till later
Consequences will be greater
Humans goin down
While the World goes round
Satan is dealin
People squealin
Tell them the truth
Tell them youth
This is the way
Believe what he say
You'll live longer
Life will be stronger
Drugs are a crutch
Jesus is a stretcher
Lean on him
and THERE he'will get ya

(Davy B)

Earlier in this book I painted a picture of a world that is out of order, not functioning as it should. I talked about teens who don't know who they are, searching for an identity and finding broken dreams and broken relationships. In this confused and harsh world where they search, some decide that something is drastically wrong and make the fatal conclusion to check out. Parents are not there; society does not seem to care. Gangs, abortion, AIDS, divorce and physical and sexual abuse is where teens live. This world needs help.

One of the biggest misconceptions in the world is that witnessing and evangelizing are things that only Christians do. Guess what? Gangs have very effective evangelists and witnesses. Musicians and entertainers do too.

These witnesses and evangelists testify and draw others to their way of life. Rock music has evangelists. They invest time, energy and money in convincing young people that they have the right program. The fornication evangelists are going around preaching every day you go to school. "Are you still a virgin, girl? Get with the program. What are you waiting on, do you want to be Mother Theresa?" They evangelize much more than we do. We are the ones who need to get with the program and stop asking why. When you know something good, you tell it to others with great enthusiasm and great joy. Haven't you ever heard your friends talk about the latest song or the latest dance move? They can't wait to tell you and show you what to do.

Jesus said that we are the salt of the earth, a preservative for a decaying and rotting world. Too many Christian teens have never been told the truth about witnessing. Some believe that witnessing is something you do when you get older. Others say to themselves, "I am not a missionary" or "I'm too shy."

The church has for a long time been a soft organization, misguided and misunderstanding its power or purpose. It has been leaving in its wake weak adults and scared teens who pray daily and hope for Jesus to come back.

I pray He doesn't come back anytime soon. I don't want to go to Heaven yet. There are people dying every day and going to hell. The devil is stealing what is ours and is trying to put us under his feet. Are you kidding? This is no time to leave. I want what is mine now. I want to enjoy this life now. God said that I should have abundant life here, so I'm not looking for the sweet by and by, or Heaven. What are you going to do in Heaven anyhow? Let's get off the Heaven trip and realize that we are here to do some positive damage.

Our commander Jesus left us here to get the job done, to tell as many people as we can tell, to share as much as we can share, to work while it is day because He wants people to know the truth. We are here as He was, to destroy the works of the enemy. No matter what the age, color or creed, the instructions are to "get busy." If you are 4 or 14, you are in the army and soldiers are supposed to get busy. Let's share the good news with those near, far, around and in between us. Witnessing is not something you do when you grow up. It's time now.

Why Get Busy?

Get busy because there was a Man who walked the earth, His name was God (Jesus), He lived and walked among us,

He went to a cross, was crucified and died, He came back from the dead and left instructions that say, "Get busy." Jesus said to go into all the world and preach the gospel to every creature. He did not ask a question; He did not make a suggestion. He said that if you are with the program, you should get busy. He never said there were options. He said, "If you follow Me, then it is your job to go into all the world and do as I told you." So get busy because He said so.

Sometimes I hear people who are not Christians say, "Leave us alone. Don't you know a person's religious belief or faith is a private thing?" Which book did they read that in? As a Christian, our Book commands us to tell others. It does not say to force others to accept what we say or to make them believe. You witness to others because you are right. If you are right, you are right. You don't have to make apologies for being right. He just said to tell them. Since He is the Master and Commander-in-Chief, we should do it because it is a part of our instructions. Witnessing is not an option, it is a command. Remember, He did not say how we should do it. He left that up to our intelligence. He said, "Just do it."

Myths about Witnessing

Many young people believe witnessing is hard. Witnessing is for grown ups; it is for "missionaries." Teens also think you have to meet a quota or that you have to be perfect before you share Jesus with others. The truth of the matter is, witnessing is not hard. (Later on I'll show some things so you can see just how easy it is.)

Witnessing is not just for "grown ups." When Jesus was twelve-years-old He was in the Temple discussing the "word" with adults. It is said that of the people in America who are saved, 85 percent got saved before the age of 19. If we wait for tomorrow, many people may never get to know the truth. If this statistic is true, then we have a serious obligation to focus on young people.

If you think witnessing is for missionaries, I have a revelation for you. A missionary is not someone who goes to Africa or who wears a long white dress. A missionary is who you see in the mirror when you wake up in the morning, if you are saved.

You are a missionary because you have been sent on a "mission from God." That mission goes with you wherever you go. There is no quota either; you do the best you can with what you have and that's it. Jesus does not carry a calculator in His pocket and count numbers. He wants you to plant seeds, and the Holy Spirit will draw the people. If you had to be perfect to witness, the disciples would all have been disqualified. Even after Peter denied Jesus and was forgiven, he was later confronted by Paul for compelling new Christians to obey Jewish laws, something Peter knew was not right. The truth is, witnessing is not as hard as we think and can actually can be a lot of fun.

Witnessing Is Fun

One funny thing is that Jesus told us to go into all the world, but He didn't say how. Jesus was smart enough to know that we have different cultures, environments, times and seasons. What will work in one place may not work in another.

Jesus told us what the message is and left the method up to us. It is our job to translate the message to our generation, to our culture and to our people.

One of the most fascinating things to see is the use of drama in witnessing. Teen Mania takes thousands of young people who may be afraid to talk or to share, but who can play a small part in a drama performed with contemporary music, and shows them how to change the world and have fun at the same time. *We must be creative.* Sometimes my young people go out in a park with rap music and drama, not in church clothes or carrying a 14 pound Bible. We go in a style and a manner that others understand.

We carry a message and not a method. Too many Christians carry a method and a culture along with the message. Find out what is fun and wholesome in other people's culture, then use the right method to reach people with the true message. You can use tee shirts, sporting events, whatever attracts young people, whatever is fun. Anything that is fun is more fun when you add the truth to it.

Get Ruthless

It is funny how the world has Christians defensive about the truth. Can you imagine us feeling guilty for being right? Never defend the fact that you carry a Bible, wear a Christian tee shirt or witness for Christ in school. Is the world sorry that they wear tee shirts with "Party Naked" or "FCK the only thing missing is U" on them? No, they wear them proudly with no apologies. We must be more ruthless about our convictions than they are about theirs. Whenever you are rowing upstream, you must be twice as strong and twice as bold. People of the world don't defend their carrying a bottle of beer or whatever because they feel it is cool and perfectly all right.

God thinks we are cool and we know we are perfectly all right, so we carry our tools proudly. Can you imagine apologizing for representing God or carrying His line of products?

People in the world think that what they do is cool; we certainly should think what we do is cool because it is. Can you imagine someone cooler than Jesus? He walked on water, spoke to the waves and came back from the dead. He invented cool. So don't be intimidated. Wherever you go in life, you are right and you have a right to be where you are and say what you need to say.

So often Christians are intimidated by the world. We shouldn't be. Look, we have a right to be here and a right to say what we want to say. God is our Father and He owns the joint, so we should not be intimidated by anyone. If they can swear, we can pray. I remember being on the basketball court one day. I didn't decide to play on a "Christian court". I went where the guys cuss and fight, proudly wearing my "message" tee shirt. As I was playing, it occurred to me that if they were going to cuss, I might as well say "Praise the Lord." I took my ball with me that said, "Love God, Hate Sin" and the word "Jesus". You see, they write words on their basketballs that express where they are coming from, so I thought I shouldn't hide what I believe. It sounded strange when they would cuss and I would say "Praise the Lord," but a funny thing happened. They began to respect me and treat me differently without my saying a word. Two guys were arguing one day and one of them was about to throw my ball in the bushes. All of a sudden the other guy said, "Don't throw that ball away, that's my man's ball. See Jesus on it?" The guy didn't throw away the ball.

Be aggressive. Don't hide your light under a bushel. We are told that we are the salt of the earth. Salt preserves things from going rotten. Let's make sure that those around us are preserved by our presence, our words and our lives. Don't wait for them to come to you and question you about why you live the way you live. Ask them why they are throwing their lives away when there is something much better for them.

The Greatest Story Ever Told

The best story you will ever tell is your own. A common misconception is that you must be a Bible scholar in order to tell others about Jesus. Some people, when they are witnessing, try to answer every question that a person can come up with. The truth is, there are many, many questions you and I really cannot answer right now. No matter how long you have been a Christian or how spiritual you are, you will never be able to answer all the questions that people have. The best thing to do is to be like the blind man in the Bible (John 9:1-34). The Pharisees came to him and said something like this: "Yo bliney, who is this dude who opened your eyes? Where did He come from? How do you know He is okay? Isn't He Mary's boy from Galilee?" The blind man had an interesting response. He said, "I don't care who He is. One thing I know, I was blind and now I see."

That, my friend, is the only thing you have to relate about your relationship with the Lord. Talk about what happened to you. You cannot speak about what happened to others, but you can talk about what happened to you: It is one thing that cannot be disputed.

Jesus did not tell us to go into all the world and answer people's questions. He said to be a witness, to describe what you have seen and know.

Your story should be: "I was once lost and in sin. I did not know or did not accept the fact that Jesus came into the world to die for me, to pay the price for my sins. He did it for the sin of man who disobeyed God and who became controlled by satan. Through (however you came to the Lord), I came to the knowledge of the truth, accepted Jesus Christ as my Lord and Savior and now live for Him. I'm spiritually connected to God. Only Jesus is the way, the truth and the life."

I remember when I was first saved I went back to witness to my friends and they had a field day with me. They would ask questions like, "Who was there before God?" "When did

God make the sun?" "Did I really believe the stories about Noah and Jonah?" "How could these things possibly be true?" I tried to answer their questions, but all I did was confuse myself further because I did not know all of the answers myself. Finally one day it dawned on me that I would be much better off if I talked about what happened to me and what can happen to them. So rather than trying to answer their questions, I asked them if they were ready to meet God, of if they needed something better in life.

The questions we have about God will never be completely answered, ever. But there are questions about God that have already been answered in your life. Concentrate on those issues: what happened to you personally, what you experienced and what is clearly supported by God's roadmap for living, the Bible. I know for a fact that I was once a confused, angry, misguided young person. I know that God turned my life around and caused me to be solid, clear and happy about life. I know that He changed me and I know that I am straight now and for eternity. I have personally discovered abundant life. It happened to me. No one can dispute that.

The Friendship Factor

Probably the most important thing you can do in witnessing is make friends. People don't believe strangers. It is fine to go to some far away country and talk to people you will never see again, but you don't have that luxury where you live and where you go to school. People you are close to will look at your life. If they can see your life lived the way it should be lived on a constant basis, that is more convincing than anything else. Also remember that people are not notches on your Bible; they have needs. Jesus was the best of all in witnessing, and you know what He did: He made friends with people. He went by the well one day and saw a lady. He just talked to her about what she was interested in and what she needed. Then and only then was He able to introduce her to the gospel.

When Jesus was around fishermen, He talked about fish. When He was around tax collectors, He talked about taxes. He went to people's homes, made friends, discussed people's needs and gained their confidence before He presented the gospel.

It became much easier to talk to the woman at the well about the gospel after He let her know that He understood how she felt and proposed a solution to her problem. If you are a student in school and you want to witness to someone, become a friend first. Play ball with that person or talk about something the two of you share in common. Talk about music, ask the person who his or her favorite musician is and why he or she likes that musician. The person then asks you who your favorite is. Use the opportunity to tell why you listen to who you listen and why you don't listen to people with ungodly lifestyles. You can invite the person home for dinner and let your new friend talk about him or herself first. Ask questions.

People love to talk about things that concern them and they want people to listen. That helps you know what people are going through or in what things they are interested. Then you can help them meet their needs or solve their problems. At some point in time, if they told you about themselves, they will want to hear about you. That is the best opportunity you will ever have, a chance to talk about your personal experience.

One thing I have discovered is that your friends may laugh at you and talk about you, but when they get in trouble and need help, they come to you for advice. So many of my former friends who told me I couldn't be a Christian and thought I was weird came to me, one by one in their individual hour of desperation and admitted, "Davy B, you have something, something special. I need help."

Plant Seeds

Many times Christians make the mistake of keeping a calculator in their pockets while they are witnessing so they can go back to church and quote statistics. "I was witnessing yesterday and ten people got saved." If you talk to some Christians and tell them that you witnessed for three weeks and nobody got saved, it is almost as if something is wrong with you. So don't count numbers. The Bible says Jesus is responsible for the harvest. You cannot save anybody; the only thing you can do is deliver the message. Once you've done your best to deliver the message, it is up to God to take care of a person's heart. The Bible talks about some planting and some reaping, but of God being responsible for the harvest.

> I planted the seed, Apollos watered it, but God made it grow. So neither he who plants nor he who waters is anything, but only God, who makes things grow. The man who plants and the man who waters have one purpose, and each will be rewarded according to his own labor (1 Corinthians 3:6-8).

Just plant seeds and share love and let God take care of the rest. Just do your best to spread the gospel at every opportunity and don't burden yourself with a numbers game. Pass out tracts, go on a summer teen missions trip with Teen Mania or Youth with a Mission (addresses for these organizations are at the end of this book). Give friends books about God and give them music with a message. Be creative. Remember, God told us to go, but He never said how we should go; He left that up to us.

Whenever you go witnessing, take a cue from Jesus. He sent people out in groups. So often we are outnumbered when we go witnessing. The more there is of you, the better. It is easier to talk to people if you have help, and it is harder for them to put up a front and be defensive if several, very confident young people ask them questions which demand a verdict. When gang members recruit, they approach prospects with force: There's plenty of us, we look like we are having a good time. Only one prospect looks unsure of himself. The argument then becomes more persuasive...you get the picture.

Why shouldn't we operate with our gang? We know for a fact that teens look for and want answers to life and there's no doubt that we have the answers. The amount of teen suicides every year tells us how unhappy and unsatisfied many teens are about life. It also tells us that they want and need help. They need us, they need the good news message. They are looking for you, your life and your example.

Points to Remember

---

1. Christians are not the only people who evangelize or witness. Gangs, rock musicians and drug dealers all have "evangelistic outreaches."

2. The church has for a long time been a soft organization, misguided and misunderstanding its power or purpose. It has been leaving in its wake weak adults and scared teens who pray daily and hope for Jesus to come back.

3. Jesus did not ask a question. He did not make a suggestion. He said, "If you are with the program, get busy."

4. A missionary is not someone who goes to Africa or who wears a long white dress. A missionary is who you see in the mirror when you wake up in the morning, if you are saved.

5. Be creative. He told us what the message is and left the method up to us. It is our job to translate the message to our generation, to our culture and to our people.

6. Too many Christians carry a method and a culture along with the message.

7. We should never apologize for representing God or for carrying His line of products.

8. Don't be intimidated. Wherever you go in life, you are right and you have a right to be where you are and say what you need to say.

9. Don't wait for people to come to you and question you about why you live the way you live. Ask them why they are throwing their lives away when there is something much better for them.

10. Jesus did not tell us to go into all the world and answer all of people's questions. He said to be a witness, to describe what you have seen and know.

11. If people can see your life lived the way it should be lived on a constant basis, that is more convincing than anything else.

12. When Jesus was around fishermen, He talked about fish. When He was around tax collectors, He talked about taxes. He went to people's homes, made friends, discussed people's needs and gained their confidence before He presented the gospel.

13. Don't count numbers. The Bible says Jesus is responsible for the harvest. You cannot save anybody. The only thing you can do is deliver the message.

9 | Redeeming the Time...

The days are evil
The Bible say
Do your work now
You still have today
Plan for tomorrow
Be your best
Spirit, Soul and Body
You'll pass the test
Don't die like Tom
Who didn't care
Just wanted fun
He wouldn't prepare
Without a plan
He just went along
It's too late now
He was DEAD wrong...

(Davy B)

The Days Are Evil

We are told in the Bible to redeem the time because the days are evil. The Bible also says in First Peter that satan goes about like a roaring lion, seeking whom he may devour. As we look around our society, we see that he could not be any more on target than he is today. The days are indeed evil. We could say that there is no other time in history when these words can be more appropriate. The days are doubly evil for youth. I have already mentioned many of the problems of today as they relate to youth, so suffice it to say that the days are evil. Some people's hearts and minds fail them because of fear: fear of tomorrow, fear of today, fear of everything. Satan has and is having a field day in devouring youth. They die every day by the bullet of a gun, the needle, suicide, AIDS. They are dying while still filled with unused potential and unmade contributions. They are full of unfulfilled promise, full of the image of God. If you are a young person today, don't be caught without redeeming the time.

Youthful Lusts

The Book of Second Timothy admonishes us to *run away from youthful lusts*. If Paul says to run away from youthful lusts, there must be some lusts that are particularly applicable to youth. Young people who look for adventure are easy prey to youthful lusts. Sex before marriage, drugs, gangs, excessive partying; these are things that "afflict" young people. The easiest time in life to waste time and spend your days pursuing lusts is when you are young. The older you get, the more settled you become and the less tempted you are by "youthful lusts."

As a teenager, you must realize that youthful lusts exist and prepare to flee or run away from them. One thing young people often don't notice is the tendency to not plan for tomorrow and to take advantage of opportunities today.

So many young people have no plan for their lives and no vision of tomorrow, so they are swallowed up by "lusts." Your greatest opportunity to redeem the time is in your youth.

Opportunities of Youth

If you are single and young, you have a great opportunity to waste time and an equally great opportunity to "cash in" or gain maximum benefit from your time. Adults who are married usually have a greater difficulty in redeeming time in some areas because a family means responsibilities that you don't have as a teenager. Make the most of your time, don't waste it. Cash in on all your opportunities, given the time you have. The parable of the talents that Jesus told could well be applied to youth. If you waste time, the little you do have will be taken away from you. If you redeem the time you have and invest it, then what you have will be multiplied. Time invested can be multiplied.

You have the greatest opportunity while you are young to read your Bible, to read good books, to work with your church and to spend time witnessing. You can also use your time now to pursue various skills in music, vocational training or athletics. Many days as a single young man I would listen to teaching tapes for hours on end. I would also listen to Christian music and read book after book on a variety of subjects. I can safely say that what I did during that period of time led to whatever success I have today. I also prayed more at that time than at any other in my life. When you get married and have the responsibilities of work and home, your time is so limited that you quickly remember those earlier days and realize what an opportunity you had to set your course positively in life. But whatever you do, take advantage of the opportunities of youth.

Three-Way Street

The Bible says in Ecclesiastes that there is a time for everything under the sun (3:1). Indeed, there are times you should allocate for certain activities and other times for other activities. If you really want to be successful, you should develop a three-way plan for your life. God is interested in your being a whole person, a person who is balanced in every area of life.

Your three-way plan requires development in three areas. First, God wants you to use your time to *develop your spirit.* Read the Word. The Bible contains the instructions for living. It is the only manual provided by the manufacturer. We must have a good understanding of our directions for life. The Bible is also our "Constitution," containing our bill of rights and orders from our President. I noticed a funny thing the other day. I saw some very young guys, who normally would be drinking beer or cussing on their way to work, on the back of a truck reading the Bible. I thought to myself, "These guys are on their way to real success." *You must pray also.* Schedule times to pray. If you want to grow spiritually, you must communicate with God in order to understand and know what His will is.

Develop your mind. Man does not live by bread alone, and he does not live by church alone either. Some young people read the Bible and pray, but neglect their obligation to develop their minds. A mind is a terrible thing to waste. The greatest battle you will fight is the battle of the soul (mind, will and emotions). It is important to guard your mind.

Therefore, I urge you, brothers, in view of God' mercy, to offer your bodies as living sacrifices, holy and pleasing to God—this is your spiritual act of worship. Do not conform any longer to the pattern of this world, but be transformed by the renewing of your mind. Then you will be

able to test and approve what God's will is—his good, pleasing and perfect will (Romans 12:1-2).

Watch what you listen to; fill your mind with things that build you up. It would be nice to sing hallelujah for a thousand if you are in Heaven, but you are not in Heaven. You are on earth, and the Bible says if a man does not work, don't let him eat. If a man does not guard his mind and develop it so that he can one day provide for his family, God says to let him do without food.

The Bible tells us to be as wise as serpents and as harmless as doves (Matthew 10:16). So do what you can to gain the most from this world in influence, money and power as a positive and not as a negative. One of the unfortunate realities of this day and world is that Jesus paid it all for your salvation, but you will pay your rent based upon what you personally have worked for! The need for money will never go away, so redeem your money.

Make yourself employable. If you want to get somewhere in life, you must plan to educate yourself and to pursue the career of your choice. Read books and magazines that are informative. Gossip magazines and corrupt novels will not give you the desired result. If you are looking to pursue a career in business, read *Business Week*. Get knowledge. God is not against college or a career. In fact, He wants people who have His heart to be in places where they can positively affect others. God wants you to be the best lawyer, accountant, doctor or computer analyst you can be. So develop your mind.

Develop your body. God wants you to develop your body! It may seem frivolous to a lot of people, but the body is very important. If you can't discipline your body to exercise or if you can't control what you eat, you may also have a problem with other forms of self control. It's better to take care of your body and exercise than it is to pray to God to heal you. The time to develop good exercise habits is when you are young, because the night comes when no man can work or when man's best years are behind him. How many older persons do you meet who express regrets at what happened in the past? They did not redeem the time. I used to run from three to ten miles a day, play basketball, swim and play tennis. That helped me make good use of extra time and also helped develop my body; therefore, I did not end up as an overweight couch potato.

So protect your body from things that would destroy it. AIDS is a big topic today and rightfully so. You can avoid AIDS by living according to God's standards. Condoms are not safe sex. Condoms are a potential time bomb; one day they might not work. AIDS kills so many young people because society does not tell you that safe sex is what was designed by the Maker. If you decide to have sex and use condoms, you are still playing Russian roulette. One day, and you don't know which one, something will go wrong and you will die a fool.

Conclusion of the Matter

The whole duty of man is to love God and to keep His commands. The whole duty of youth is to love God and to keep His commands. If you love God and keep His commands, you will live and not die. Anything else is folly, as Solomon would say. Be determined to make it no matter what background you come from. Once you have received the Word, set your course. The greatest bunch of bull I ever heard is that Christianity is so difficult. The rain falls on the just and on the unjust. It is much harder to live your life trying to recover from drug abuse than it is to follow Christ and be free. Being a Christian is easier, better and more rewarding.

Young people need to know the truth. The truth is that in the long run, it is always easier to do it God's way. In this life you will have trouble, but the just are on a rock; the unjust are on sand. How can you fail when you are on the rock? We may all make mistakes, but don't condemn yourself, there is so much life ahead. God forgives and gives second chances; you ought to give yourself a second chance if you fall or fail to reach the mark. Never get tired of doing good. Never get tired of being right. Live your convictions. So many adults and young people are too wishy-washy; if the wind blows, they go with it. We need warriors who refuse to bow to an immoral society that has little or no integrity. I have seen life from both sides of the fence: the wrong and the right. God's way is much better. Young people need to know that His way is much better. You are tomorrow's leaders. It is up to you to decide what the future will be...Go West. Peace (from the Prince of Peace). DB.

Note: If you have never made the decision to commit your life to Jesus, the best time to do it is now. All you need to do is say the following:

Jesus, I realize that You came into this world to die in man's place and to redeem him from sin and separation from God.

I confess that my life has been lived separated from You in a sinful state.

I ask You to come into my heart and life and make me new.

Forgive me of my sin and give me a new start in Your grace.

This day I accept You as my Lord and Savior and I will follow You all the days of my life.

Amen.

Now remember to go to a Bible-believing church, pray and find all that is full of life and answers for youth based upon God's Word.

It's the only way...DB.

Teen Mania
P.O. Box 700721
Tulsa, OK 74170-0721

Youth With A Mission
P.O. Box 55309
Seattle, WA 98155
Tel. (206) 363-9844

RELEASING YOUR POTENTIAL, by Myles Munroe, is the exciting sequel to the best seller *Understanding Your Potential*. Discover how you can release the powerful potential God has created within you! Drink deeply from the wells of living water that Christ has deposited within you. TPB-168 p. ISBN 1-56043-072-9 Retail $7.95

UNDERSTANDING YOUR POTENTIAL, by Myles Munroe, helps you to discover your awesome potential. Learn how God has deposited His enormous power within you. Join thousands who have seen the Lord unlock their potential with this book! TPB-168 p. ISBN 1-56043-046-X Retail $7.95